The Rest of Us

ALSO BY JACQUELYN MITCHARD

The Deep End of the Ocean

JACQUELYN MITCHARD

The Rest of US

Dispatches from the Mother Ship

Viking

For Sean and Michelle—above and beyond—
and, always, for Jo

VIKING
Published by the Penguin Group
Penguin Putnam Inc., 375 Hudson Street,
New York, New York 10014, U.S.A.
Penguin Books Ltd, 27 Wrights Lane,
London W8 5TZ, England
Penguin Books Australia Ltd, Ringwood,
Victoria, Australia
Penguin Books Canada Ltd, 10 Alcorn Avenue,
Toronto, Ontario, Canada M4V 3B2
Penguin Books (N.Z.) Ltd, 182–190 Wairau Road,
Auckland 10, New Zealand

Penguin Books Ltd, Registered Offices:
Harmondsworth, Middlesex, England

First published in 1997 by Viking Penguin,
a member of Penguin Putnam Inc.

1   3   5   7   9   10   8   6   4   2

"The Martha's Out to Lunch," "One Carpool, Minus One Mom,"
"Rude and Unusual Punishment," and "True Tales of the Kissing Patrol"
were published by Tribune Media Services. © Tribune Media Services, Inc.
Reprinted by permission.

The other selections in this book first appeared in *Ladies' Home Journal*,
The Milwaukee Journal Sentinel, and *Parenting*.

LIBRARY OF CONGRESS CATALOGING IN PUBLICATION DATA
Mitchard, Jacquelyn.
The rest of us : dispatches from the mother ship / Jacquelyn Mitchard.
p.   cm.
ISBN 0–670–87662–3 (alk. paper)
I. Title.
PS3563.I7358R47   1997
814'.54—dc21   97–28786

This book is printed on acid-free paper.

Printed in the United States of America
Set in Palatino
Designed by Jessica Shatan

Acknowledgments

What my life as a writer and a person has turned out to be is a group project, and I'm no more responsible for the words in this book than any member of the team who made it possible for me to sit down and write them.

I want to thank the "first eyes" on fully half these essays, my late husband, Dan Allegretti, who was a true friend and a good writer. Hats off to the crew chiefs: Susan Pschorr, Karen and Lili, and the Saturday girls, Mol and Mer. My family, who helped hold the fort on this one, Brian and Janice Mitchard, Robert and Sandy Mitchard, my daughter Jocelyn, and the godparents, especially Stacey, Chris, and Jean Marie, deserve commemorative T-shirts. So do my colleagues at the *Milwaukee Journal Sentinel* and Tribune Media, including the light of librarians, Linda, who kept faith, and especially my first newspaper boss, Elliott Maraniss, who let me write my first column—which he hated—and my second, which he didn't hate as much, and who finally taught me the knack of writing some he didn't hate at all. Bless my children, including the littlest, Francie, who passed her first year thinking that every day was "Take Your Daughter to Work" day.

No language is large enough to thank Pamela Dorman, Barbara Grossman, and New Jersey's own Patricia Kelly, the Vikings who somehow thought I could be a contender, as well as the goddess of line editing art, Beena Kamlani, for her amazing grace. And though I may have been standing behind the door when great hair was distributed, I was blessed with three people's share of remarkable friends: Franny, Sandy,

Laurie, Anne D., Hannah, Amy, Kahlil, Ken, Linda, Louise, Shaina, Shira, Emily, Deb, Hilary, Kate, Georgia, Judy, Sylvia, Steve, Bill, and Leonora are just the tip of the iceberg that stands steadfast between misery and me.

For their generosity and steadfastness, I wish to thank the staff, board, and directors of The Ragdale Foundation, in Lake Forest, Illinois.

And then there's Jane Gelfman, my dear comrade, who taught me to spell agent this way: "a-n-g-e-l."

Contents

Introduction

It's a peculiar feeling, this, writing an introduction to a book of my own essays.

It's kind of like inviting a crowd of strangers to my house for dinner, but meeting them at the door to explain why they shouldn't make fun of the furniture.

Collecting these essays made me think of paging through a photo album of snapshots, not just of past events, but actually of previous selves. Science says that the body replaces its entire population of cells in seven years. That's the body of time these essays cover; and in my case I can feel the fact. I'm another person entirely from the one I was when most of these pieces was written—different down to the molecular level, living the world through another lens. And yet these snapshots of the person I once believed I'd always be are mine, too.

When I began writing these essays, I was a securely married mother of three, expecting a fourth child. Times were lean, but my newspaper-editor husband and I had hammered away many of the twists and traps of early married life and hit a smooth stride. Through a long struggle with infertility, the unexpected joys of adoption and birth, and a series of family cataclysms, I wrote everything I could to support my family—from criticism to cover stories to speeches for Donna Shalala, who would become the longest-serving cabinet secretary in presidential history. After my husband died, young and quickly, from cancer in 1993, I wrote with even more urgency and purpose, those of a suddenly single and financially strapped mother. I started my first novel, *The Deep End of the Ocean*, at forty, and it was published in 1996 with the kind of success that blew open the doors of my professional life.

Only one thing never changed. I never stopped, not once, even for a week, writing my beloved newspaper column, "The Rest of Us," which followed me all the way from my Cosmogirl period to the years of early motherhood, from a stomach that I prized for its concave contour to a stomach I prized for its cesarean scar. My column was my constant. It served as the springboard for essays I later wrote for magazines and for stories I later wrote as fiction. I kept it in my hip pocket as I navigated from deserts to high sunflower fields in my career, and through the narrow straits of new motherhood when I decided to adopt a baby girl on my own, past moral crossroads of loneliness and new love. I first wrote it for Madison's *The Capital Times* and then for the *Milwaukee Journal Sentinel*, and then in syndication for Tribune Media.

But I never changed the name, though by journalistic etiquette I should have. I always wrote "The Rest of Us" with a secure knowledge of my audience. "The Rest of Us" was me. Now, for the first time, I have to try to explain what that name means—both to those of you who have read my essays and to those of you who never have.

Let me propose the Melody Knoll paradigm.

Melody Knoll lived across the hall and one door down from me when I was in college, and it wasn't because she was beautiful and superbly confident (though she was) that I watched her like a movie.

It was that she *knew*.

She knew she wanted to be a physical therapist because it was socially relevant and yet well-paying; she knew how to find the best, sanest, gentlest guys, and was never even tempted to drive past their houses at midnight to see if they were home. She seemed to have been genetically endowed with the ability to approach any system in a clear and supremely pragmatic way—from faculty advising to sorority rush to her checking-account balance. Melody understood, when her peers were wondering if there was vitamin C in Thunderbird, the importance of regular exercise and lots of water. She told me that my wrists would not break out in hives every night over calculus if I began looking at the problems as logical puzzles, instead of slamming the book closed in horror before I even read them.

As an adult, I began to realize that there was more than one Melody in the world—that, in fact, there were a great many. They *knew*. Some of them knew the political answer, and some the health answer, and some the romantic one. Though I have always wanted to be or marry such people, I would not dare write a column for them.

I can't help but write for the rest of us. These are people like me, who alternate between the absolute conviction that we could, if need be, save France, and the desperate uncertainty about whether to get out of bed on a given Tuesday. Who believe wholly in the concept of a good, free, modern, public infrastructure and yet want to blow up the sewer system when we get our tax bills. We have strong moral cores, but waffly ways. The question "So, would you rather be good or be happy?" can give us pause every time. We're just not entirely *sure*. But we can see that the world always seems filled with emperors running around naked and not enough people willing to yell and point.

When I read that men arrested for domestic violence were able to get their guns back for deer-hunting season, I had to write about that. When I read that Martha Stewart, bless her heart, suggested that parents individually stencil their children's lunch bags in seasonal colors to make them more creative, I had to write about that.

Many men have written to me in thanksgiving over the fact

that I am not their wife. Many teenage young women have written me asking me to call up their mothers and intercede. Many grandmothers have written to me that I will eat my words someday, and I've already dined on a few.

Even when it seemed no one would take my opinions in print even for free, "The Rest of Us" remained a reliable haven—somewhere—for the things I somehow cannot bear not writing. It helped me survive hard times and comprehend them, as a mother and mentor, worker and daughter and friend. When things got better, there were good reasons—among them time and money—to give it up.

"Quit," a friend advised once. "They pay you chicken feed."

"Not true," I told him. "A chicken couldn't live on this."

So now it's not the money or the bylines that keep me at this, but the fact that I would be as unable to quit writing down these few intemperate words a couple of times a week as to stop breathing in and breathing out. I will likely be in the middle of some teapot tirade when they find me slumped over and have to scrape off the moss.

If writing novels is my chance to conduct the symphony orchestra, then this other kind of writing is my six-string guitar, on which I pluck out the simplest of melodies, those closest to the core. If this book never existed, and if all my newspapers dropped me like hot tar, I still might well go on writing the column only for me, and probably for free.

But I hope, too, that it's also for thee, the rest of you, who, I know without being told, sometimes want to shout out loud and sometimes want to ache in quiet, just as I do.

Because in the end, the rest of us isn't really me at all, it's you, it's all of us.

Do Pigs Go to Heaven?

On Catching a Dream

WHEN my husband, Dan, was a boy growing up in Chicago, he used to have a recurring dream: He'd be on the roof at Comiskey Park, the home of the Chicago White Sox. You hear stories about batters hitting home runs onto the Comiskey roof, although that's really happened only a few times in history. But in Dan's dream, home runs were hit up there all the time and they fell around him like apples from a tree. He stuck them in his pockets, and when his pockets were full, he stuffed them in his shirt.

In real life, although he went to as many baseball games as possible, mitt in hand, he had never caught a ball. And lately, he was as likely as not to leave the mitt in the car and just enjoy the sunshine and the game.

Two years ago, on a bright spring Saturday just this side of sunscreen weather, we set out for Milwaukee's County Stadium to see the Brewers take on the Kansas City Royals. It was the first time all our children—a girl and two boys—were old enough to last more than two innings. We sat in one of the designated family sections, about six rows back, between third base and the outfield wall. "Watch out when it's a left-handed hitter," Dan earnestly told our little tribe. "Those balls can come in pretty hard where we're sitting."

No sooner had he spoken than a ball, a high looper, came soaring toward us. Dan held his breath and waited hopefully. But the ball curved away to hit the bleachers just in front of where I sat with our toddler in my lap. There was a melee of spilled soda and windmilling arms. A college kid emerged

triumphantly from the fray. He held the baseball aloft for admiration, then tossed it to a seven-year-old boy sitting nearby
whose longing for the ball was almost visible, like a cloud
around him. "Hey!" we all called. "Classy move! Nice guy!"
Then we settled down for the rest of the game. The kids soon
lost interest, and the two oldest amused themselves by recov-
ering unsavory artifacts from under the seats. But not a half
hour had passed before, incredibly, another ball smashed into
our section, hitting the concrete about two feet from me. A
bald fellow one seat over hit the deck and snatched it up. I
looked over at Dan and was astonished to see his lips pressed
into a thin line.

"What's wrong?" I asked.

"Nothing," he said.

"No, what is it?"

He explained, reluctantly. "See, it's just that if I had been
sitting where you are, I'd have had that ball. Not that I'm
blaming you or anything." He said he understood that a
woman would not throw down a baby even to scramble for a
foul ball. He sat back in his seat with a sigh.

It was the fifth inning, and the Brewers' shortstop, Dale
Sveum, a switch-hitter, was coming to bat. "Okay," Dan said
to the children, "he's batting left-handed. Watch your heads
now." But since the kids were under the seats foraging, he
didn't press the point, and that's when we heard the smack of
the ball.

It was a hard line drive. Dan rose to his feet. He said later
that his first thought was, It's going to pass me. But then he
saw it curve, and he started to silently chant, "It's coming, it's
coming."

No time to reach for a mitt. He just stared up into the sky at
the scuffed little sphere descending, drew a deep breath, and
held out his hands.

It landed, with a satisfying smack, right in the chest-high

pocket formed by his hands. There was no scramble, just an awed silence. No one else had even had a chance to try.

The silence broke. "Did you see that guy?" the bald-headed man shouted to the crowd. "He did that like he does it every day. Buddy, that was some catch!" Our kids squealed, "Daddy! Daddy!" Little boys crawled down from the section above to touch the ball. Strangers slapped Dan on the back.

But Dan was quiet. He took a pen out of his pocket and wrote on the ball: "May 1, 1988. This was caught at my son Danny's first ball game." He let our children hold it, his own hands framing theirs as if they held not a ball but a fragile egg.

The catch was particularly well-timed. It came along shortly after Dan had turned forty, and the prospect of middle age had been pinching him like a pair of new shoes. But now he had bare-handed a line drive off the bat of a major leaguer in front of his kids and his wife, and it restored him. For months to follow, there was a lightness in Dan's step when he recalled the moment. It was a gift straight from baseball into the hands of a grown-up boy who used to haunt the roof of Comiskey Park in his dreams.

Guys and Dolls

WHEN our oldest son, now seven, was two years old, a relative gave him one of the Cabbage Patch dolls, then at the apex of their popularity. Our son's doll was named Alexander Kincaid or something. But he quickly was rechristened Tony. And Tony he remained.

Since crib days, Tony has spent a lot of his time propping up a shelf or snuggling with the dust moozies under Bobby's bed. But recently, after Bobby's newborn cousin visited and Bobby had spent a great deal of time caring for her, he got Tony out and gave him some fathering, changing his clothes and tucking him in.

Then, one Monday morning, Bobby announced that he was taking Tony to school for sharing time. I wasn't paying much attention and said, "Okay. Stick him in your pack."

Bobby answered, "That's not too nice. I'll just carry him under my arm with my book." Meanwhile, Bobby's father was making vigorous throat-cutting motions over Bobby's head.

He pulled me aside and said, "Don't let him take the doll to school. You know what will happen." And then Dad exited, stage right, leaving me with this bomb in my lap.

Paying full attention now, I looked at my blond-haired son, cheerfully spooning up Cheerios while Tony leaned against the cereal box. I knew that in my own youth a seven-year-old first grader who brought a doll to school (under his arm, no less, a doll wearing a sleeper, not camouflage!) wouldn't have survived to the end of the block. Times have changed, I thought, but really, how much?

"Honey," I began gently, "if you take Tony to school, some of the kids might tease you for having a doll."

"Why?" asked Bobby. "They have bears and dolls, too."

"Well," I said, "in the olden times, when Dad was little, boys played with trucks and trains and soldiers, but they didn't have dolls."

"That wasn't too fair. How did they practice being dads?"

Good question, I thought, and considered. Do I tell him, Well, Bobby, back at the beginning of the second half of the twentieth century, there were very different ideas about what constituted male role identity? But I said, instead, "I guess their wives taught them when they were grown-up. Or their moms did."

That cracked Bobby up. He practically spit out some chewed Cheerios. As Bobby packed Tony up, I thought, should I tell him it's fine to play with Tony at home, but only at home? Would that mean to him he had something to be ashamed of?

Were we now going to give Bobby the message that gentleness, unlike throwing a ball straight, was not an activity for public consumption?

All that day while I worked, I thought of my kid, the potential laughingstock. I worried that Bobby might come home in tears. But he didn't, didn't mention Tony until I asked. Then he told me that the only one who teased had been Jeannette.

Some of the little boys sort of liked Tony, I surmised. In any case, they didn't seem to find Bobby weird.

But did I? Did my own upbringing make me expect him to turn into he-man once he got out of training pants? If so, why? We didn't raise him that way. Still, it took some getting used to.

Now I see Bobby's choice in taking Tony to school as not only a matter of guys and dolls. I think it was a gesture of trust. He trusted our judgment in letting him have his doll. And he trusts himself now. And if only for that alone, I think he will be a very good father someday.

Little Men and *Little Women*

ONLY one of them, my five-year-old son, was literally kicking and screaming. But even the two older boys were nervous as we entered the theater.

"I don't see many young boys here," my son Danny, eight, commented judiciously (and correctly). "What I mostly see are grown-up women with their friends or teenage girls."

My eleven-year-old son, Robert, slumped down in his seat. "I don't know whether it's better to move away from you so people think I'm alone, or sit with you so people know my mother made me come."

The night was Tuesday. The year, 1994. The film? *Little Women*. Okay. Okay. I know you can push this gender-neutral stuff to a fault. But, I argued persuasively, girls as well as boys would be going to see Macaulay Culkin in *Richie Rich* (a movie about a boy).

"That's a good idea," Robert suggested. "Let's go see that, next door."

"What I meant was, so why can't you guys see a movie about girls?"

"It's not just a movie about girls," Danny explained. "It's a girl movie."

I remonstrated with him. *Little Women*, I told him, was perhaps the most important book of my youth—didn't he want to know why? There were very funny and sad and wonderful parts in the movie. The girl from *My So-Called Life* was in the movie. Couldn't he at least try to enjoy it?

He frowned.

"Anyway," I pointed out, "I'm paying." They extorted the promise of milkshakes afterward if they did not enjoy the coming two hours.

And then the classic story of four girls growing to adulthood during the Civil War years in New England began—as tender and true as it ever was. My children's rapturous attention was proof that though Louisa May Alcott might have crossed over into preciousness in some of her lesser novels, her masterpiece still stands against anything as a portrait of adolescent longing, the evolution of ethics, the anger and forgiveness that test and strengthen family bonds. It was a movie that did more than I've ever been able to do to convince my sons that girls, when they're alone, act more or less as goofy as boys do when they're alone. That the differences, while real and even profound, are not incomprehensible.

And when gentle Beth died, the only one not crying was my littlest, who kept whispering, "Ma, she's really not dead. She's on Thursday nights on ABC." After the show, when I was still crying, I remembered my mother reading *Little Women* aloud to me, reading me the part in which Professor Bhaer breaks Jo's heart by telling her that she should write from her heart instead of writing about vampires and ghosts. I remembered how that amazing, simple advice went straight to my own newborn writer's heart and took root there, and then my son Danny said, "I get why you liked the book."

"Why?" I asked him, as we piled into the car.

"When you were a little girl, you thought you were Jo," he said.

"I did," I told him happily.

"And you had the same initials," my son Robert put in. "Did you know that?"

"Did I know it?" I exclaimed. "Back then, I thought it was a sign that I should grow up and be a writer."

"So," he said, with much more charity than a preadolescent boy dragged to a chick flick should be capable of, "maybe it was."

And nobody even mentioned the milkshakes.

A Stand-up Mom

DON'T get me wrong. I'm not the kind of woman who scurries to clear the table at Thanksgiving while the men get out the cards and cigars. But sometimes I do something I swore I never would: I stand while the rest of the family eats dinner.

I don't exactly stand sentinel, circumscribed by an apron, but I lean against the kitchen counter, sipping a cup of tea while my husband, our teenage daughter, and our three young sons chow down. And sometimes I wish that my own mother could see me this way because long ago, when she did the very same thing, every particle of my budding feminist consciousness would bristle.

In those days I believed that my mother's standing during dinner was a symbol of everything I'd never be: the second-class household citizen required by odious tradition to put everyone else's needs first. What I didn't know then was that my mother had it all figured out. Once I became a parent myself, it didn't take long to discover that dinner with the family could be an occasion for more quease than ease. Not because our three-year-old customarily dips his vegetables in his beverage; I'm used to that. No, what churn my stomach are the constant near-misses, the teetering cups, the flash of gravity-defying cutlery. Then there are the endless requests for more milk, a clean spoon, another napkin to mop up a spill. Why take a seat, I ask myself, only to stand again, and in such a rush that a person could pull a hamstring?

I once thought that when my fantasy children chirped,

"Mom, milk please!" I would say, gently and firmly, "There's milk in the refrigerator. Please get it." Now, I realize that my children will gladly get their own milk. They will even be careful to pour it over the sink so that the quart they spill in order to fill a six-ounce glass will not hit the floor. A five-year-old dispatched to bring back a clean spoon will bring back six—as well as a rolling pin and several food-processor attachments.

I suppose that sitting calmly and regally at the dinner table isn't the only ideal of fantasy motherhood that has been dashed over the years. It's just one item on a long list of things I swore I'd never do: I'd never allow myself to be referred to as "Mrs." anything, never pick up my husband's underwear, never park my children in front of the TV so I could make a phone call, never screech at them through clenched teeth to get a move on, and never call a child stupid for messing up my clean house.

And, indeed, I never have called a child stupid for any reason. But the rest of these things, which I once believed defined the mother-as-harried-servant, now just seem to be the way a family (even a nifty, fifty-fifty family) works. Still, I don't believe I've really abandoned my standards: I've just expanded them. And I'm more tranquil for it.

Yes, I do have a right to sit at the table. But I have a right to sleep through the night every night too, and sometimes that just isn't the way things go. What my mother knew and what I've learned, is that sometimes you put other people's needs first not because you have to but because you want to. My mother told me this once. I'm sure it's just that my head was probably too high in the clouds to hear. Now, feet planted firmly on the linoleum, I can see that just as I didn't like classical music when I was young because I didn't have the ears for it, I couldn't understand the pragmatism basic to parenthood because I didn't have the maturity for it.

So there's no point in sharing my dinner-hour advice with my own daughter, who sometimes gives me a sidelong look when I swoop down to replace the empty bowl of applesauce before pandemonium erupts. Nope. Let her sit while the sitting's good. The relative merit of being a stand-up mom is something that only reveals itself in time.

No Time for Lamb Cakes

I drive past the happy women a couple of times a week. They are all about thirty-two years old; they are slender; they have good, straight, thick hair; they are a little pregnant and have one or two toddlers clinging to their knees.

When I drive past, I feel guilty. Not only am I usually supposed to be somewhere else and running, but I feel like a voyeur. I often wish I could stop and watch the happy women invisibly. There is always something to watch. One woman is pulling weeds, with a child sitting nearby. Two women have pulled their folding chairs together on the driveway and are drinking tea while their offspring play.

Privately, my friends and I call such happy women "the saints." This is not meant unkindly, but I think of it as self-defense.

It is not only that these women have made the pretty courageous choice not to work outside the home while their children are young—that's not the half of it. They look to me, as I rush by with my days clenched between my teeth, as if they also know how to revel in family life in ways I do not.

They are the kind of women who make oatmeal "sandboxes" in big baking pans for their children on rainy days, and then don't yell if the kids grind the oatmeal into the rug.

They look like mothers who could take their toddlers to a museum and doodle all day with Legos and block stamps, the way children love to do, without worrying about getting home in time to make one call or get dinner cooked.

They probably have Crock-Pots that have been out of the

boxes. They probably wait patiently while their five-year-olds mix muffins without itching to grab the bowl and scrape the blueberries down off the sides.

The other night, my eight-year-old's best buddy stayed over, and when he was going to bed, he showed me a fabric bear he and his mother had made that day. They just up and made it that day; she cut out the pattern, and he and his sister chose the decorations.

Though I complimented that bear and honestly admired it, I also felt a pang. I never made my son a bear. I sometimes think I never made my son anything but nervous.

I wonder if my mother noticed the happy women. She was happy, in her way, but unusual. When I griped that other mothers made lamb cakes for Easter, she told me, not angrily, "Well, the first thing you'll need for a lamb cake is another mother."

She did not seem to have big, goofy concerns about how her children would remember her. I do, however.

Years ago, I read Gypsy Rose Lee's memoir of her mother (the inspiration for the Broadway show *Gypsy*). At one point, someone told Ms. Lee, "Gee, your mother must have been awfully nice," and the daughter of brassy Mama Rose had to wonder. "Nice? Charming maybe. Even gallant. But nice?"

Will my kids remember me as nice? Gentle? Or something more uneasy, like "interesting"?

Of course, there is very little percentage in wanting your children to remember you in ways other than what you are.

Yet I wince when I think of my grandchildren hearing about the time Mom set the towels on fire trying to dry them quickly, or the time she let the kids wrap the whole outside of the house in yarn that cost $3 a skein. And yet, those were funny times—if not precisely middle-American. My kids love those stories.

And when I recall them, I am, I suppose, in my own befuddled way, a happy woman.

Loneliness of the Long-Distance Talker

I heard about the phone bill even before I saw it. It was a phone bill of heroic legend, $90 of talk sandwiched into a one-night, two-day weekend between our daugnter and her sweetheart at college out in the Wild West.

I remember talk. I remember about fifty different kinds of social talk I indulged in as a girl/woman.

There was plotting-revenge talk. It began without salutation or preamble: "Did you hear what she said?"

There was talk-to-set-up talk: "He called Billy and told him he wanted to call you, so do you want me to call him and tell him he can?"

There was date-dissection talk: "What did you do when he did that?" (There is an evolutionary form of this talk, boss dissection: "What did you do when she told you that?")

Mourning talk, there was a great deal of mourning talk: "I can't believe it's over. It seems like I just met him yesterday. . . ."

And then there was the most puzzling form of talk—the really weird form—talk conducted while you were doing something else. While you were watching television, or talking to someone else, or doing homework, or fighting with your father, you kept the line open. It was like sitting beside one another: you observed each other's lives through a wire.

Women's relationships to the phone have changed between my own time and my daughter's. We dared not call a boy. You've heard of the magical thinking that arose from this un-natural prohibition: Driving home and counting the number of lights you caught—more than five, he'd have called. Fewer than five, you'd have to wait. The games people played: calling his number, just briefly, for a nanosecond, not long enough for anyone to pick up, to make sure the phone worked. Waiting in agony, holding it instead of going to the bathroom, because no sooner would you shut the door than the phone would ring. Finally going out with your girlfriends to the pool, finding out later he'd called twice.

My daughter calls boys. Young men, that is. She doesn't scruple about calling, twenty-seven times, by my phone bill tabulation, in one afternoon. She calls, unless they've had a fight, and then all bets are off. She slips back into the waiting state of a previous generation. She is hamstrung. She cannot make the first move, even to tell him off.

It is uncanny, this thing about women and phones. Studies show that men control the use of phones; phones most often are listed in their names, they decide who can use them and when. But women answer them. Women make the call. "Call the neighbors and ask if I can borrow the lawn spreader," my husband would say. I would make the obligatory protests, the same ones I made when he asked, "Where's my raincoat?" But then I'd make the call for him.

All of the best news and most of the worst I've ever received came over the phone. It's the most powerful instrument in my life. And I don't hate it, as some do; when I come home from a weekend and find thirty-four messages on my machine, it's like a gift.

The only thing that troubles me is that I have passed phone dependency on to our daughter. Our son recently found out about his stolen bike; someone left a message. He wrote down the number and meandered off.

"Aren't you going to call?" I scream. My daughter did the same; we'd have sprinted over coals. But Bobby was doing something; the call could wait. At that instant, I really understood the X-chromosome phone link. I envied him his self-possession.

I made the call.

Dare to Say
"Underwear"

I did not hit my stride in the underwear area until I turned forty.

It never occurred to me that fancy underwear would actually fit better and last longer than the fistfuls of $2 garments I would grab out of a bin while waiting in line to buy aspirin and juice boxes.

Once I understood that, I decided to buy some from the neat underwear catalog, from which I'd never ordered anything but blue jeans.

And so, charge card in hand, catalog open to three sets of underwear in colors that would not have looked out of place in a display of flavors at an ice-cream stand, I called the fancy-underwear vendor.

A guy answered.

Now, on a scale of 1 to 10 in terms of bluntness, my friends assure me that I am a 15. I say what is on my mind, a habit my mother often remarked might eventually cost me several front teeth. Friends have actually sent their seven-year-olds to my house so that I can explain to them where babies come from.

In other words, not much embarrasses me. But when the guy at the fancy-underwear catalog asked me what my first item would be, I said, "Jeans." Having thus bought a pair of denims I didn't need, I steeled my nerve.

After all, I would never see this person face to face. There is absolutely no reason why a person of the male persuasion should not be working as a telephone-sales rep for women's underwear. I suspect, even, that there are women who might have found the situation amusing—though I would like to meet and interview one who could have bought the see-through lacy black chemise on page 8, in the same situation, with a straight face.

All I was buying, I reminded myself sternly in the eternity of seconds it took for me to name the next item, was ordinary clothing. Stuff every woman wears. There's no reason I could not say "Bikini briefs, medium," to a total stranger in another state. Nonetheless, having gotten past the underpants, I used a serial number to identify the next purchase.

"That's a bra?" he asked.

And I died several thousand deaths before I muttered, "Uh, yeah." He then asked me what size.

Now, I'm a widow and nobody would identify me as a neighborhood goddess. My friends' husbands are shocked, when I wear a dress, to see that I actually own stockings and high heels. As far as I can recall, my own husband never knew what size my underwear was. And here I was, about to confide that to a total stranger and ask for it in persimmon.

The salesman was perfectly at ease. He knew all the lingo, padded and unpadded, wires or none, and asked about each in excruciating detail. He told me what the specials were. I wanted to put a pillow over my face.

At last, however, the journalist in me asserted herself, and before I hung up, I asked the young man, "Are folks surprised when it's not a woman who picks up the phone?"

"Oh, yes," he said.

"What do they do?"

As it turns out, they do a lot of things. Some hang up. Others tease him, and make the purchase a giggly little source of flirtation. Still others, like me, seem to view the experience on a level of pleasure roughly equivalent to flossing their teeth, and simply proceed with grim determination to the conclusion.

"Do you like the work or does it embarrass you?" I asked him.

"I have four sisters," he said. "Why should it embarrass me?"

Why indeed? Why should it embarrass me? Out of all the hang-ups in the world I could have, this is probably the most inane. Would I want my sons to grow up unable to talk about underwear, too shy to buy it for their wives? Of course not.

And so the next time I have to order underwear, maybe I can get one of them to make the call.

An Elf Is Just an Elf

I had a sort of argument the other day with a friend about arts and crafts. Actually, it was crafts we argued about.

There was this old magazine lying around in the house of my friend (who is both artful and crafty), advertising something like "500 Spectacular and Easy Holiday Gifts You Can Make for Under $10 with Things You Already Have Lying Around the House—Most Likely in the Recycling Bin."

And you can guess the kinds of things they were: Holders for things that already come in holders, like facial tissues or cotton balls. Things that you can walk outside and see, like branches and twisted vines. Then there were the really crafty ones, like pomanders made of quilted fabric squares and stuffed with (homemade) potpourri.

They were pretty things. And even the quilted-fabric-square pomander probably would cost less than $10 to make in sheer material terms—though the labor would probably come to, for me at least, about seventy hours, which, even at minimum wage, would make a little closet brightener more expensive than any gift I've ever given anyone for any occasion. Like more than my wedding ring cost, for example.

And all I said was this one little thing. I said, "Can you imagine if they had magazines like this for men?" My friend got a trifle huffy. "Well, they do," she said. "*The Home Carpenter* or *The All-Around Handyman*. Those are the equivalent." I didn't say anything for a moment. I was admiring an elf made of felt glued to an empty liquid detergent bottle (liquid detergent bottles were very big items in this multipage feature story).

And then I started the argument, telling my friend that, no, those handyfolk mags were not the same thing at all, because when you completed fixing the light you had a repaired light and not a detergent-bottle elf, an elf that was only decorative—which is what I think people who make up plans for elaborate busywork crafts for women think of women.

"What," asked my friend, "about guys building shelves or something in their garages?"

Those are shelves, I replied. You can sit something on a shelf. Like a book. Or a detergent-bottle elf. Which, even if beautifully made, will be no better or worse than any other detergent-bottle elf. "Or any handmade shelf," she said.

"A shelf is still a shelf," I told her.

Then we got down to it. What about crocheting afghans, she asked. Or quilting blankets for babies that get passed down to their babies and their babies? Well, it's my opinion that those are folk arts and of a higher order or endeavor, a true calling—even if you do it badly—compared with silly make-work things that would be valuable only for third graders learning small-motor skills.

I think that craft projects are created by people who don't think women are busy enough (we are) and that we need something to occupy our tiny minds and hands. My friend sniffed. "Oh, heck. Don't make a social issue out of it. Can't something just be nice for its own sake?"

Well, sure. But I'd argue that every moment spent on making a detergent-bottle elf could be more beautifully spent reading to a child, even your own. And I did argue that, but then we let it drop, because I actually like ornaments and place mats and stuff. I'd just prefer to buy them from people who make money on them.

And I still think that if people tried to sell a guy a magazine about ten terrific gifts he could make for me with wire and felt and glue, he'd roll it up and throw it at them. Because even if men don't have better things to do with their time, they think they have better things to do with their time. And I think women could, too.

The Martha's
Out to Lunch

WHY spend energy railing against the tobacco lobby, health-insurance costs, and the politics of personality when we have The Martha?

Ordinarily, I simply regard Martha Stewart with the same awful thrill I get when I accidentally flip the dial to pro wrestling. There are times when all of us, no matter how hard we try, feel sloppy and tasteless—and it's a comfort knowing that there are things going on out there that can make you feel like a Cabot or a Lowell.

But the other day, The Martha crossed the line, in an essay about packing school lunches for children. Now, by conservative reckoning, I have packed six thousand school lunches, and I would cheerfully have the hairs on my legs tweezed one by one to avoid ever having to pack another one.

Why? It's not the lunch itself but what the lunch represents—yet another operation, yet another obligation, and perhaps most of all, a sort of textbook example of the way parents' best intentions meet with children's determination to avoid them at all costs.

Martha sympathizes. She knows how easy it is to fall into a dull routine. Actually, though, she chirps, school lunches can be full of surprises.

Actually, though, ours generally are surprises, for me at least. Consider the reappearance of the lunchbox mistakenly left at school for the weekend or the semester. Simply throwing out the thermos is not enough. It is necessary to throw the thermos out in Oklahoma. Even lunchboxes that come home daily provide a little message—empty Ho-Hos and Gummy Bats wrappers that give us hope that our children, who set out with turkey on rye and carrot sticks, have a future in commodities trading.

Theoretically, my children are supposed to pack their own lunches, and they do, with the same vigor and commitment they bring to tending the litter box. Asked to include basic food groups, my eldest packed a full squeeze bottle of Cheez Whiz and two chocolate-chip granola bars. There are obviously things parents are better off not knowing, yet I did ask whether he had put the Cheez Whiz directly on the granola bars.

"Of course not," he snapped. "I just squirt it right into my mouth."

My ten-year-old pointed out he could no longer bring fruit in his lunch. "The grapes kept getting in other people's shirts," he explained.

Cruelly, I once insisted the children eat "hot lunch," even though I knew that I was subjecting them to horror-combos that can make even children cry: such as bean dogs and mango gelatin. "I'll just take a piece of bread," my second grader begged after a week. "Just plain bread."

What Martha suggests is personalizing. Good stationery stores carry an impressive array of rubber stamps and colorful inks, she writes, adding, "Bright colors and metallic ink look good on brown bags." This reminds me of the time I had to fax my friend a story from a parents' magazine suggesting such brown-bag offerings as sprout-and-hummus enchiladas. I wanted to read it aloud to her, but I was helpless with laughter.

For The Martha, characteristically, it's all in the packaging. Use paint pens and paper cutouts coated with clear varnish to spruce up a plain lunchbox. Change the color schemes on cookie bags—such as green for St. Patrick's Day.

Picture it. "Honey, can you run out for a gallon of milk and a couple of pale pink clear cellophane lunch bags? I'm personalizing for Valentine's Day. I'll clean up the orange stuff the dog spit on the rug and cut some pictures out of *Architectural Digest* while you're gone."

Well, you already suspect the truth. Either Martha Stewart never packed a school lunch in her life or she's having a big old jolly joke on all of us.

However, just for the record, I do personalize. Only one of them likes jelly.

Going beyond that would be the equivalent of cleaning the Augean stables to stock up on fertilizer.

Just FYI, Martha. Some matters require a grim toughness of mind, and school lunch is one. Would we presume to tell you how to stencil your driveway? Please show us the same respect.

Do Pigs Go to Heaven?

IT finally happened, during a dinner that included—because it was made up of leftovers—two kinds of meat. Danny, our four-year-old son, paused reflectively between bites of bratwurst and asked, "Is this dead?"

Gentle reader, we ignored him deliberately. Even those people who eat meat, as my husband does, with relish—"and with ketchup and mustard," he adds happily whenever I say this—don't like to talk about it with their children.

Meat, like a few other things in life, doesn't bear too close an inspection.

I don't eat it, though I remember being forced to, a couple of times, as a tot. It's not because of any nouveau health concern. Usually, however, our dinner table is not so meaty as it was this night, with both bratwurst and steak. And Danny, who has an affinity with anything animal, asked again, "Is this dead?"

"It's, yes, it's cooked meat," said his father briskly.

"But is it dead?"

"It's dead all right," his seven-year-old brother, Bobby, informed him with gusto. "It's dead and cut up. Dad is this a dead and cut-up pig or a dead and cut-up cow? Dad?"

"Pig," my husband murmured quietly, giving me an icy look that said plainly, If you tell him that this bratwurst might once have been a fluffy little lamb you will face a fate very similar to this bratwurst.

"Oh," Danny said, putting down his fork. "This is sad. This pig is dead. Was it a baby?"

I remembered the horror with which both my husband and I had looked at a jar of puréed veal we'd accidentally picked up on the baby-food shelf about six months before.

"You can't feed a baby to a baby," my husband said. "Even I wouldn't do that, and I think humans should eat meat."

We put it in the back of the cupboard, to be eaten in a natural disaster.

Now my husband said quickly, "No, it was a daddy pig, Danny, and it was near the end of its life."

"A daddy!" Danny cried. "What about his kids?"

"They ate them, too," said Bobby with an evil smile.

Danny asked for more applesauce. Then he asked softly, "Is the pig in heaven?"

"Pigs don't go to heaven," said his father. "Pigs are for eating. . . ."

"Wouldn't be much of him left for heaven!" Bobby put in, to a general "Hush up!" from all.

"Do doggies go to heaven?" Danny asked, then, urgently.

"Yes," I said. Another furious look. I shrugged. Danny looked hopelessly confused.

I don't blame him. It's hard to sort out. We wouldn't eat a bottle-nose dolphin, but we'll eat a cow, which probably, in its simple way, had just as much going for it as any lissome sea mammal.

Don't eat anything that has a face, say the veg folk. But what about shrimp? They may not be lookers, but you certainly can tell which way a shrimp is pointing. At this age, Danny doesn't seem to think fish have much of an interior life. He eats them without thinking.

He's too little to understand high and low food chain. He didn't eat his bratwurst. It was ruined for him. I don't know whether to feel guilt or sympathy.

Maybe, given the way he is, Danny will stop eating meat as he grows up. Then someone will tell him, How about drinking milk, from cows that are forced to keep breastfeeding for years?

Well, the way I figure that is there are worse fates. The lot of cows in life is to work for people. But there ought to be limits to what a creature—even one whose entire vocabulary is "Moo"—has to do to keep her job.

Honey, It's Not Over Till I Say So

THERE'S a look I see on our daughter's face some-times, when she looks at me or her father. It's not disgust—she's too sunny and decent a person to feel disgust. Call it horror.

We're old to our daughter, old, old. Not old as rocks and trees, like her grandparents, but too old, except for sentimental reasons, to live. She can't understand why we would do such things as, oh, wear shorts and expose our knobby, chicken-soupy-colored legs.

When we tell her that she is making a future date with skin cancer by lying out (she calls it "laying out") in the sun from 10 A.M. until 2 P.M., she looks at our legs and says, softly, that she'll risk it. I know exactly what she feels. There's no way on earth I could tell her that.

She isn't as obvious as our younger children, who some-times ask us brightly whether there were cars "in the olden time," when we were children. But we get the hint from over-hearing conversations that she has with friends: "She looks so old, like she was twenty-five or something."

We can tease her, but our teasing can't dislodge what are, to her, facts that we can no longer bear to face. To her, twenty-five is old, thirty-five is old, and forty-five is beyond imagination.

I met a researcher in the field of aging recently, and she told me about big, national studies that had been done regarding the way younger adults—people in their twenties—apprehend the feelings of older adults.

Many of the younger people, it turns out, believe older people must feel pretty miserable. After all, they can't "do" anything. Their big-earning, child-raising, rock 'n' rolling days are over. Their world is small, circumscribed by their limitations.

In fact, however, older adults feel pretty happy, these same surveys show. They feel wise, seasoned, satisfied. This is something I have a hard time grasping myself, even though I'm way past twenty.

Right now, I'm on the extreme nether edge of what might be called youth. That is to say, I could still, if money and inclination and ability were factored out, have a baby or write a screenplay or become a lawyer. In a few years, some of these possibilities will fall away, forced by the gravity of longevity. When I think of how I will feel then, beached on a narrowing shore, it's hard to be terribly hopeful.

But what I know and what our daughter Jocelyn cannot, yet, is that you adjust.

If I were to tell her how wonderful it feels just to sit on the porch at night and listen to all of the kids, upstairs and supposedly asleep, kidding and calling to each other, she would roll her eyes. If I were to tell her that it is restful to know that certain things, like romantic heartbreak, can be survived, she would think that being in love, like great thighs, was just another thing I had ceded to time.

I wish there was a serum I could give Jocelyn (and perhaps I could use a dose of it, too) that would imbue her with the understanding that life is not a steady upward progress to college and then a steep decline.

It might ease her fears, if she has any (she doesn't; fear is not in her vocabulary). It might let her know that, in that void ahead, there are compensations, the kind we enjoy from having her and her brothers to care for—and perhaps, later, from not having them to care for.

I want to tell her, You're right, it gets worse. No drug, no job, no amount of money is ever going to allow you to feel as sheerly alive as you do now. But it also gets better. What you think of now as love you someday will think of as bubble gum compared with sweet, ripe fruit. I could tell her that.

But it would be like telling her to stay out of the sun.

It's a Jungle Gym Out There

THE way to the bank goes past my older son's school, a nice public school with much of what parents think of as the right stuff: family involvement, committed teachers, and manageable class sizes.

As I drove past, I saw children outside for recess. Two kids were fighting. The bigger one was kicking the other boy in the stomach. Three others were jumping around the edge of the fray. Farther along the fence, two other children were locked on the grass in what looked like mortal combat, one pummeling the other on the head.

Absorbed as I was in trying to determine whether this was roughhouse or war to the knife, I wasn't able, even at the speed of twenty mph, to take in the entire playground. But I didn't notice anyone over four feet tall anywhere about.

Perhaps instants after I drove past, teachers rushed in to break up the fray. Perhaps the kids were only playing around and not really hurting. But what I saw looked like unsupervised nine-year-olds beating each other silly.

And so I drove slowly to the bank, trying to figure out how to draw out enough money to finance our son's tuition at a private school run by Swiss nuns with only five children to a class.

What I remembered was the terror of the schoolyard. I hadn't thought about it for years.

The memories included big boys with rocks in their fists, their teeth the size of ice cubes. A row of jeering girls, aged about eight, only a year older than I was, powerful and nonchalant in their unity. Walking past them in my ankle socks with pandas on the cuffs was like running the gauntlet.

"Did Mommy put those on for you?" they taunted, just under the level of the general roar. No teacher could hear. I was too embarrassed to tell my mother.

I remembered far back, to kindergarten. One of my first memories was of the other children locking the door on the teacher as she returned from taking a phone call. Locking the door and trying to push the piano in front of it. (What kind of school did I go to anyway?)

Was I the only one who couldn't breathe, who wanted to rush out the door and hide behind the teacher?

There always were *those* kids. Not really first-tier baddies, not the ones whose parents kept the chair in the principal's office warm. These cool kids made decent grades, but they weren't classroom stars. They didn't give a rip for authority, but even teachers admired them.

They were popular. Grade school was the first time I understood the seriousness of that concept. Confidence shone from them. Their word was schoolyard law.

I look at my own little son, who is beautiful as an angel and runs fast, but also is complicated and bossy and bookish, and wonder what the in crowd will do to him. Not for the first time, I think over all of the choices we made raising him.

No Nintendo, nothing on TV more violent than a Warner Brothers cartoon. Building sets instead of G.I. Joe. He is what he is: a comic who would rather argue than throw a punch.

That day and the next, I made phone calls to small, sensitive schools. But even as I pored over the materials they sent, I knew on some level that our son was going to have to endure the terror of the playground, wherever he went, face it alone, try to make coalitions as best he could. We would have to close the door and our mouths when we heard bolder kids torment him. We could wrap our love around him but not hide him inside it.

Having decided to keep him at his neighborhood school, however, didn't soothe me. A part of having children is reliving the pure pain of learning that people hardly ever want you as much as you want them to. It passes. You heal. But it never stops hurting. You just go on to bigger playgrounds.

Love on the Hard Shell

IT'S a painted turtle, Mom!" said Danny, three.

"It's not just an ordinary turtle!" said Bobby, six. "And we saved him. We saved his life from under the wheels of a car. We're going to keep him, Mom. Turtles can live a long time."

It looked like a painted turtle, all right, just about the size of a man's hand. We made a hole in the sandbox and filled it with water, and Skipper—why are turtles always named that?—sank down into the makeshift pond to the level of his eyes and floated there, evidently not much impressed with his new digs.

Bobby and Danny began discussing Skipper's future (whose school he would visit first, whose bed he would sleep in) while their father and I exchanged long looks over their heads.

The matter of pets comes up weekly now. It's been two years since our golden retriever threatened two kids, ate one couch leg, and exited, stage left, to the home of a bachelor. The older kids' grief was sharp and short, but Danny, who was no more than a baby when Jesse-the-dog left, still mourns.

"Why don't we have another dog, Mommy?" he asks in honest puzzlement. "He can sleep in my bed. I'll feed him grass."

Danny's such an attacher, such a caretaker, we feel as though we're somehow contravening this little kid's destiny by not getting him a dog. But we're almost scared to, for the same reasons. What if it bit? What if it got hit by a car?

Still, each time he pleads, we think: When the children

wake up on winter nights, we don't have to take them outside. They get jelly on the curtains, but they don't chew them. I'm allergic to cats and home wouldn't be home with even one salamander in it. Birds don't know who you are. Fish are like houseplants. A dog seems like the only pet you can talk to, and one day we might get back into the dog business. We're too tired now.

So, for the present, Danny is so pet hungry he names ants.

"We'll think it over," I said of Skipper the turtle.

We called a pet store and spoke to a turtle maven, who gave us the bad news. To stay healthy, Skipper needed everything but a health club and winters in Palm Springs. An ultraviolet light to start, mounted in a twenty-gallon aquarium, and a rock vacuum for his rock. Old Skipper would need about $150 in supplies. Even the children understood that we couldn't do it.

And then their nanny, who felt guilty about bringing Skipper home in the first place, told them that there weren't as many painted turtles in the world as there should be.

"He needs to go back to the pond and have a family," she said.

"We're his family," Danny said, and Bobby nodded wistfully.

But the next day we liberated Skipper, giving him a taste of raw hamburger, which he thankfully condescended to eat, as a parting gift. At the last instant, Danny burst into tears. Then Skipper raised his head and swam off. Danny said, "Did he wink at me?"

"He'll remember you," our nanny said.

"Turtles don't have memories," said Bobby.

"They do, too," said Danny.

Right from the start, it seems that life lets you in on the notion that much of what we do is to let go. School ends and friends scatter. People move away. Pets pass through our lives. The whole business builds toward the towering realization that almost everything—even lakes, even you—is more or less temporary.

Danny said one night, "He winked at me. He thinks about me underwater sometimes."

Turtles might not have memories, but people do. And I don't know if this makes it easier or harder.

My Son the Warrior

UNTIL now, we took a fair amount of pride in the fact that we could raise boys we described as sturdy but gentle. Boys who could throw straight but also liked to cuddle, and who made guns from their breakfast toast only occasionally, not every day.

Then along out of babyhood came our youngest son, now rounding the curve toward age three, and we have to admit we think this boy is an alien life form.

Martin, who has been raised exactly as his brothers have been raised, sleeps with a plastic scimitar tucked into the band of his training pants. He sidles up to the couch evenings, and with a beseeching look in his big almond-shaped brown eyes, says, "Mommy, may you fight with me please?" He often carries two swords (spoons will do in a pinch) for this purpose. And so I sit, desultorily whacking away in mortal combat with my toddler, who crows when he lands a direct hit, "You're dead now, Mommy. Please fall over."

I know that Martin loves me—after all, he must depend on me to give him food since he is too short to reach the cabinet handles. But when I hear him sing his version of his favorite song, "Ol' McDonald had no mommy, ee-ay-ee-ay-oh. . . ." I am unsettled. And recently, he performed a Freudian maneuver that was an even greater source of consternation.

We have a children's wooden crèche next to our Christmas tree, and we had visions of making it work in the style that

French families do—you know: The Three Kings (called the "Wise Guys" by our sons) start out a few feet away from the manger and move a little closer every day throughout Advent.

Martin took an interest in the crèche this year, and I noticed immediately that every night at bedtime, Baby Jesus was on the roof of the stable.

"Why is he up there, Marty?" I asked.

"He's hiding from his mommy," Martin explained with his customary intensity. "She always tells him no, don't do that. He can't stand her."

This, I thought, is an angry young man. And I get further evidence all the time that Martin is the toughest cookie in our jar.

The other night, I was helping him put on his pajamas—an indignity he no longer suffers gladly. Taking pity on his restless cries, I soothed him, "There, there. You're Mom's little puppy. . . ."

"No!" he cried. "I'm king of the wild frontier."

I suppose it is difficult to be king of the wild frontier and still have someone count out the carrots on your plate. Martin's nature brings home to me again and again the truth that our sons and daughters are only passing through. At first, they are of you, born to come to your arms. Rapidly, they are with you, pausing only long enough for you to dab a few hurried strokes of paint on the canvas they are becoming—they are on their way to belonging to themselves, and then to the world. If we are lucky, they always will consider our home their harbor, but they are headed out to the open sea, almost from the first.

I sit tonight, looking at Mother Mary, her head softly bowed as she waits inside the stable for her little son to get over his fit of pique and come down from the roof. And I think of thousands of years of mothers of growing children who bowed their heads and hoped for the best, as they wondered, What child is this?

Lost: One Best Friend

IT wasn't anything he said, or did. It was just that my eight-year-old son's natural sunniness seemed . . . dialed down, somehow, over the past few weeks. And then, one day, he walked in, kicked his shoes into the corner, and slumped into a kitchen chair.

"You look like you just lost your best friend," I said. He turned to me with tears in his eyes. In fact, that was exactly what had happened. I wanted to shove my fist in my mouth.

Bobby's best buddy had broken the news. He didn't want to be "best pals" anymore. He had another special friend he wanted to spend more time with. And he didn't appreciate Bobby's showing up at the door every morning expecting to walk to school, either.

Well, I think I said all the right things. I told my son this had less to do with him than with his friend. People change. Life doesn't always feel fair. Other friendships would come along.

But all the while I was saying this, I could feel a bruise growing inside. Of course, this had to happen. The two boys had been joined at the hip for the best part of two years. They had done everything together—Scouts, sleepovers, visits to each other's churches.

It was just such a good relationship. The parents were fine people; we shared some essential ideas about what children should and shouldn't do. Shoot, I thought, it's too soon for all this again; it seemed we'd just gone through the cycle of tears and jeers and tense back-and-forth phone calls that attended the settling out of our daughter's preadolescent friendships.

"I guess he thinks I'm a real jerk," Bobby told me.

"I'm sure he doesn't," I assured him.

You big fibber, I thought. Of course he does. Or, at least, you feel as though he does, and that's the same thing. You can't lose a friendship you cherish without experiencing that old shiv to the ribs: rejection and its sidekick, doubt. As I fell asleep that night, I found myself unable to get the lost friendship off my mind, found myself getting angry at the other child, at Bobby (perhaps he'd been inconsiderate), at nasty fate.

It took a day or two for me to ask myself the question: Was I so upset because I was mourning for Bobby? Or for me?

I realized that the more Bobby told me about the hurtful little exchanges that led to the demise of his friendship, the further I hurtled back, thirty years ago and yesterday, to when I was the same age and learning firsthand what is perhaps the most painful truth of the human condition: not all people like you, not even when you like them. It runs like a minor-key refrain through every other relationship in life, from work to love to living in a neighborhood. How you handle it determines how well you'll handle the ups and downs of everything else that comes your way.

I had thought I handled it pretty well, until I cast myself headlong into the current of identification. It didn't take a psychiatrist (though I probably could have used one) to figure out that in Bobby's loss I saw the need not only to protect him but also to patch up those other old wounds, for good.

Fortunately, however, Bobby seemed to take me at my word. Though he grieved, he came to see this loss as bad luck rather than bad karma. He got busy with other friends. He made himself a kite. He was more philosophical than I ever was long ago.

Okay, than I am, still.

All the Little
Live Things

WE were barely settled after arriving for a week's visit with friends in Washington, D.C., when it became apparent that their nine-year-old son's hamster, Hank, was headed for the big aluminum exercise wheel in the sky.

That may sound comic. But the situation actually was pretty grim. Like many modern kids with mobile parents, our friends' son, Zachary, unable to have a big dog or a furry feline, transferred all that affection seeking to Hank and Nerissa, his pals in the neighboring cage on the laundry-room floor.

Now Hank lay in extremis with a back injury of unknown origin. Of course, Zachary and his sister, Jessie, six, could think about little else.

My friend Gayle, Zach's mother, and I stood down in the laundry room that night, languidly sorting clothes as an excuse to debate Hank's fate. Every instinct we had, as human and humane animals who could sympathize if not empathize with Hank's pain, told us to do Hank in. But how would we? How could we?

Most suburban households don't come equipped with ether or deadly and fast-acting poisons. The conversation rapidly took a macabre turn: Aspirin? Would it work? How much? Vodka? Car exhaust? Call a vet? At midnight?

We know that if Hank had been a wild hamster he'd have been dinner for a predator by now. If we'd been rural instead of city-bred women, we could have taken a more sensible line. If Hank had been a field mouse, we'd have cringed at setting a trap for him. But we'd have done it.

But this was a rodent of Gayle's acquaintance. "And, on top of that, I just don't know if I can set out to take a life," she said.

Of course, that started the whole discussion. Hadn't the family just that day eaten food made from animals who probably have richer emotional lives than Hank's? Where was he, after all, on the big continuum? Below a dog? Above a fish?

Were there *kinds* of life at all (yes, we agreed), and was Hank's level of awareness a factor (yes, we agreed again, a little nervously). We talked about euthanasia, abortion, animal rights. It was interesting talk. But Hank kept breathing. "So what should we do?" Gayle said.

We went to bed. Hank would have passed on by morning.

But he hadn't. Not that day or that night. He got worse, sicker, not even stirring. On the third day, Gayle and I, fed up with our anthropomorphic timorousness, dispatched him gently, but so thoroughly that we had to devise a hamster mummy from a beanbag and a piece of cloth. The unsuspecting kids then laid this Hank effigy to rest under the big tree where others of his tribe had gone before him.

"This is why I resist getting my kids pets," I told Gayle, who answered that this was actually part of why she did get them pets. We stood there uncomfortably, watching our children play in the yard. "I just don't want to be surrounded by things that are so fragile," I said.

"But you already are," Gayle said.

She bought a new hamster (Nancy) later that day.

A few days after we'd left, Gayle called to tell me that Zachary began crying hard one night in bed. "It's Hank, it's Hank," he said. "I can't get over it." She murmured comforting things, about the good times, about the end of pain. Zach seemed momentarily comforted. Then he began to cry again. What is it? his mother asked. "It's death, it's death," Zachary said. "I can't get over it."

I'm with you, kid.

Give Them a Mile and
They'll Go the Distance

YOU let these kids get away with too much," my brother says, not reprovingly but with a kind of sympathy.

He thinks, because I am single, that my children run over me a little. This makes him feel bad. When I ask for specifics, he points to all the rocks in front of my house.

Oh, those, I think. I scarcely notice them anymore. But I can understand how other people might.

They're gold, after all. You could see them from Saturn.

My two older sons spray-painted them. It took two cans; I was out of town. It was intended as a surprise for me. "Now," my son Danny explained blissfully, "everyone will think that we're rich."

The big gold rocks do look a bit out of place in my placid neighborhood, where gunmetal-gray shutters are considered a kind of bold departure from the earth-tone norm.

My brother could probably offer other examples, as could others too well-raised to comment. They might mention, perhaps, the fact that, if we have to get up extra early, I let the children sleep in their clean clothes overnight. Or that I let them eat ice cream on their bran flakes in the summer because they have convinced me it's the same as whole milk. Or sleep in my bed if they get scared.

Right now, my oldest son has a sixty-three-foot strand of musical twinkle-lights strung over the bookshelves and around the window in his bedroom. I hear it, softly beeping, "It Came Upon a Midnight Clear," as I fall asleep. He says it feels like being in a greeting card.

It's not that my children don't have boundaries. Two of them were discovered ferret tossing; and though they were only two feet apart and the ferret was not worse for wear, they suffered consequences. They're stopped from hitting, swearing, and watching too much TV. They're compelled to eat raw vegetables, do their homework, and learn to read music.

Beyond that, I think they feel they're making it up as they go along.

In the admonition "You let these kids get away with too much," the key word is "let." Their eccentricities and demonstrations of independence aren't something I want to stifle.

My maternal grandfather was one of the most congenitally life-loving people I've ever met. I never knew his mother—simply that her name was Alice Adams and she was called Al. However, one of my strongest memories is something my grandfather told me, when I was very young, about his mother. She had five children and lived in a railroad flat above a city street too dangerous for the youngest children to play on. So each day my grandfather and his brothers and sisters would pile all the pillows from the beds on the floor and bounce from couch to couch and then onto the pile of pillows. They did it for hours. "What would Al do?" I'd ask him.

"She'd laugh," he told me.

Even more so than today this was probably considered letting kids get away with too much.

And yet they all grew up strong and straight and never got in any trouble. They may have ruined couches, but they didn't ruin their lives. Allowed to act crazy and immoderate in small ways when they were small, they (this is just a theory) didn't feel pressed to act crazy in big ways when they were older.

Truly, it drives me nuts when my son Martin makes a paste of chocolate syrup, baking soda, crushed corn flakes and glue and freezes it. But he thinks it's fun, and he appreciates the freedom to do it. So I bite my tongue and try to pry the natural cement out of my coffee cup a few days later. Maybe it won't make any difference later on, but I'm betting on the wisdom of my foremother Al.

I'll let you know how it goes.

My Angels in the Outfield

MY husband used to boast of me. Not about my cooking or my writing. He was the envy of his friend because he had a wife who, even if alone in the house, would watch baseball.

Though I certainly cannot match statistics about the '69 Cubs with the truly religious, I was raised on baseball. From the time I was six until about twelve, I was part of a neighborhood baseball game that started on the last day of school and lasted the entire summer (final score: 451–382).

When he was a young man, my grandfather was a pitcher with one of the Chicago Cubs farm organizations. All this by way of saying I loved the game. You will note the past tense. Even Ken Burns couldn't revive baseball for me after the strike, and I was willing to be placed on a respirator. When I read of big-league team management expressing "real disappointment" over the low fan turnout this year, or more of Bud Selig's endless harangue about the fate of civilization hanging by the thread of a new stadium, I wonder if those who run the national pastime really understand that basketball has seized its position as the game that expresses a nation's poetic imagination.

Even my late husband, who really did think life imitated the World Series, would have believed, as I do, that professional baseball has finally flatlined, at least for fans of my generation. But what about forever?

The other night, I endured, in ninety-degree heat, the short-stuff equivalent of the May 9, 1984, game between the Chicago White Sox and the Milwaukee Brewers. That game lasted a period of two days, eight hours, and six minutes. My son's game took a mere five and a half hours, but it felt like the duration of Marla Maples's engagement to Donald Trump. The skeeters were ravenous, and the younger siblings amused themselves by drooling into hills made of dirt and then rolling on them.

And yet, it was there, during those long moments, that the sweetness of baseball made its way back home to me. It has always seemed to me that the magic of baseball is not only in its gentleness, its reliance on skill and savvy rather than brute force, but in its reliability as fantasy. A boy who'll never be taller than five feet nine or who's chubby or slow cannot picture himself wearing jersey No. 23; but he can picture himself wearing Lee Smith's California Angels cap.

There are certainly players whose talent is a divine gift, but almost anyone can learn many of the skills that stand out on a baseball diamond, at least well enough to enjoy. Almost anyone, gender notwithstanding.

On my sons' teams are boys and girls who have lightning legs and boys who have to whack one over the trees to get to first base. Children who have glue on their mitts and children who seem to have ball repellent on theirs. But there is room for everyone.

The hottest slugger in the battery on my younger son's team is named Brittany. On my son's friend's team, the catcher has an artificial leg. As I watched all of them, stretching for that one sweet fly ball catch, digging their toes into the dry dust, sliding into third, I thought that perhaps baseball is only shedding rotten branches at the topmost levels. That the trunk has strong life in it yet. That perhaps the reclamation of this good game will draw sustenance from the intensity of Josh and Tyler and Tiffany and Alex, not from the kind of fans who can't see except from a skybox that costs $10,000 a night to rent.

I'd rather watch the Shopping Channel during these seasons of strikes and other greedy foolishness, but perhaps by the time my children grow up baseball will have its head on straight. Or perhaps its heart.

Where the Deer and the Squirrels Display

IT was my children's idea, going to this restaurant that people in town had told them was real "North Woods." To me, that meant a place without a no-smoking section, but hey, it was vacation, and I was game.

Game is the key word here. When you go to restaurants in the North Woods, you often see evidence of the taxidermist's art. More evidence than you'd see anywhere south of the Klondike, I'd venture.

I'm not wimpy, and I don't blanch at every glassy-eyed deer I encounter over a mantelpiece. But this place, which shall remain nameless, rocked me back on my heels. It was an animal necropolis. Even my kids, at first fascinated, soon felt the weight of karma lie heavy on their prime rib specials.

I would defy you to go into this restaurant, pick out any vantage point—high, low, or in-between—and be able to find fewer than five stuffed animals in your line of sight. And I'm not talking teddy bears. The bears in this place ranged from toddlers to full-grown—some mounted by a taxidermist on all fours, some standing up straight.

One wore a cowboy hat and one a Packers' jersey. There was a wildcat reclining on a large stone ledge, surrounded by all its kits, which might have been a tender scene except for the obvious.

There were geese, elk on the hoof with antlers as wide as the hood on my car, a great horned owl and a not-so-great snowy owl, a wolverine, a coyote, and, probably most disturbing of all, two timber wolves.

"I thought you couldn't shoot wolves," my son Danny, eight, said softly.

"Maybe they died of natural causes," I told him.

My son Robert, eleven, noticed the newborn fawn mounted in a grazing posture under a table. "Who'd shoot a baby deer?" he asked.

"Uh, natural causes," I said.

But how was I supposed to explain the otters, the mink, the ferrets, the chipmunk?

"How would you even shoot a chipmunk if you wanted to?" my eldest son asked.

"With a very small gun," one of his brothers replied.

And then there were the comical constructions—the two-headed calf; the squirrel aiming a bow and arrow at one of his luckless brethren.

One wall was dominated by a wreath made of a pheasant and all its feathers. The feathers formed the spokes of the wreath, the luckless bird's head was the centerpiece. Dead-bird crafts.

"That one definitely died of natural causes," I said hopefully. "Otherwise, it wouldn't have been all . . . in pieces."

"Or an AK-47," my eldest son put in with mordant cheer.

We weren't able to get out of the place without touring the back room, where more exotic trophies were displayed: polar bears and African animals, moose and foxes. And of course, everywhere, there were trophies of all manner of fish that ever breathed water. Even the coat racks were made of animal horns.

The chairs were, however, plastic.

When I confided to my children, later, that this place gave me the creeps, they assured me (they are, after all, guys, and know what to say to a woman) that I was overreacting.

They reminded me that one of my favorite haunts, the Field Museum in Chicago, boasted exhibits of creatures that were actually human beings. And furthermore, that people I knew and respected were hunters who brought hand-killed meat to their family tables.

I couldn't argue. But I was reminded again why the North Woods, much as we love it, seems like a parallel universe in the same small state.

I was also glad I ordered the salad bar.

When You're Out
with the In Crowd

I just had to yell at my thirteen-year-old son for talking on the telephone too long. It was such a relief I can't tell you.

Our daughter was so sought-after she could have used a social secretary by fifth grade. But her brother is another story. Smart and insecure, shy in a way he covers up with bombast and sarcasm, he'd spent a record two years without a single birthday-party invitation.

Now, I wanted to give my children the same lessons you did yours: Don't follow the crowd. Pay the most attention to the opinion of the person in the mirror.

And yet there have been moments when I would have cheerfully eaten all those idealistic words with ketchup to spare my children's hearts. I can summon an instant headache recalling the time my son ran into a playmate hosting a party at a local pizza parlor. "Hi!" my son said, smiling. "Why didn't you invite me?"

"Only smart people can come," the friend said, leering.

"Kids," said his mother, rolling her eyes at me over her son's head.

My reaction was cool and measured. I wanted to blow them both up.

Analyzing why I react so passionately when my children experience rejection might take a psychiatrist. Then again, Sigmund Freud's receptionist would spot instantly that I was a teenage outcast. I was the equivalent of Pluto in the social galaxy until age sixteen or so—when the feminist movement gave even girls permission to have opinions and most of my body parts finally came into alignment. Even then, I was only a renter in the suburbs of popularity, not a permanent resident.

Of course, having eyes and ears, I could tell that Roxanne Milette looked like Pizza Waitress Barbie and had a voice like a busy signal. Even before I understood Darwinian theory, I couldn't figure why all boys wanted to be her crush and all girls wanted to be her best friend. I could tell that her charm would be short-lived, and that I would come into my own long after Roxanne's firecracker had fizzled; and this, in fact, was true, because the last time I saw her she was selling hairbrushes from the trunk of a car.

It never crossed my mind that my children would experience friendlessness. Even TV sitcoms that are supposed to be about new-kid hell end up with everything peachy keen within the first twenty minutes. You don't come to this with a whole lot of resources. So I told my son my own story. He just looked at me and said, "So you're saying if I wait thirty years, everything will be all right?"

Being wanted is the tender heel of everything human. And in the end I guess I was telling my son that there was no alternative to simply staying yourself and hanging on until the competition got winded.

I've wavered—I've actually considered telling my son to try to observe other kids and do the things they like to do. But that would have been tantamount to advising him to just say yes—to trendy computer games today and cigarettes and beer tomorrow. More important, he really bought all that stuff about marching to a different drummer. And so do I.

Nonetheless, the other day, when I saw that my son had to use two sheets of paper to write down the phone numbers of all his friends, I wanted to go out into the street and buy roses for passing strangers. It was true. Some people have to grow into their personalities. When they do, all is well.

And then I remembered I have three more children.

Out of the Mouths of Babes

THERE'S a jokey tradition at our house about the Tooth Fairy.

The original tale goes something like this: One day, a neighbor came by to see my friend Hannah. Both women had little girls about the same age. Both girls were sporting recently acquired gaps in their smiles.

Talk on the porch turned to the moola that good children found under their pillows the morning after they lost a tooth. Karen got fifty cents. Francie got a dollar. Karen got miffed. "Don't you know," she said loftily, "that the Tooth Fairy is really your mother?"

Hannah's child turned to her with mournful puppy eyes. "Is that so?" she asked, and Hannah, feeling that bittersweet way we do when something tender and silly ends, began to nod. But the other mother suddenly spoke up.

"Yes," she said firmly. "Your mother is the Tooth Fairy. But she's the Tooth Fairy for everyone."

Over the years it took to fill a jewelry drawer with tiny teeth, we've enjoyed a certain cachet: after all, the Tooth Fairy—by day, a very serious government official—is a member of our extended family.

Then my middle son, Dan, turned ten a few weeks ago. Dan's funny. He's been shedding childhood illusions along with baby teeth the way he does most things, a little more slowly than most. I'm not sure why. Children usually froth at the bit, counting the years until they can have a driver's license, sparring with their folks over the justice of the R movie rating.

Dan doesn't even ask. Though he does scorn certain things (such as bib overalls) as "too babyish," he chose not to see *Batman Forever*. When I asked why, he said, "I just knew it would gross me out." Pretty brave and independent in most ways, he seems quite content to linger in the cartoons-and-Legos stage of life for a little longer than most of his peers. I've worried about it a little, embarrassed on his behalf, wondering how those peers would treat him if he'd seem like a mama's boy without tough-guy ways.

He lost a tooth in summer, and, for the first time in my motherdom, I actually forgot that Hannah really wasn't going to take care of this for me, and Dan found nothing but a tooth beneath his pillow.

I pulled him onto my lap, intending to give double cash as consolation and a gentle session on how pretending isn't just like lying. But before I could, Dan said, "I think Hannah must have gone to Washington, like she does sometimes. She'll probably take care of the tooth tonight instead."

I searched his face. No guile, just wistfulness. I realized that he knew, and had long known, who really engineers surprises at our house. With a pang, I also realized that he was doing this for me. He thinks that by growing up he's letting me down. Should I tell him so? Urge him to grow up, lest others make fun of him?

I tested the waters. "It's possible," I said.

He smiled widely. "Anything's possible. It's okay to be late."

Well, I guess it's okay with me, too.

True, Dan's peers are mostly already miniteens, with hip-rider baggies and earphones. But nature didn't make them that way, merchandising did—capturing kids' natural longing for power by pushing the trappings of adolescence, from spicy CDs to Joe Camel caps.

Dan likes to peek at the underwear catalog, too, but there's still only seventy pounds of him, mostly legs and dreams. And if all the things that kids learn in school about tolerance for individual differences are true, then they should extend to different rates of blossoming. Maybe Dan's timid about growing up, but maybe he simply, rightly sees that all those adult privileges have a price.

Anyhow, I'm not going to be the one to rush him down the road. Ten is universally considered the end of early youth, the threshold of adolescence. If Dan wants to stretch his last moments of protected space, I'll protect his right to do so, and so will our close personal friend, who moonlights by tucking crisp, new dollar bills under the pillows of children who wait.

Pencil Me In, Son

I had a date the other night with my son Danny. He's eight and a half. He wore his only-for-school-pictures shirt, and I wore my speech-making coat. We went out for crab legs at a restaurant distinguished for its kiddie cocktails, dawdled over dessert.

We talked about Danny's plan to gather a team of second-grade detectives to prove that the small green footprint outside the girls' washroom at school was left by a leprechaun. We talked about critical issues of lift and drag in the construction of paper hang-gliders.

But mostly we gazed into one another's eyes like honeymooners. "We're the quiet ones," Danny told me. "I'm glad we had some private time together."

It was Danny's idea, this date of ours. He rightly self-identifies as the quiet one, though in a family a little less loud than ours tends to be, his reticence probably wouldn't stand out so much. I'm not quiet by anyone's standards, except when I'm with Danny. His peace modifies me in magical ways. The other evening when Danny came to kiss me goodnight he said, "I want us to go out alone. How about Wednesday?"

Without thinking, I asked him, "Do you want to go with friends and their children?"

Danny fixed me with a look: "Do you know what 'alone' means?"

And I had to reflect: Sometimes I wonder whether I do know.

I've always believed that, if you have more than one child,

it's important to make each sibling feel like an only child, at least once in a while. But belief doesn't always translate into practice. For a single parent, squeezed by the urgencies of making a living and making a life, the hours between sunrise and sunset flip past like those calendar pages in old movies.

When Danny suggested our Wednesday date, I nearly demurred. Wednesday's the only night I have a regular sitter. It's Mom's night out—or alternatively, Mom's night to work. "You know that I keep Wednesday nights for me," I told Danny.

"Well," he said. "I thought of that. But I go to bed at eight o'clock. So you'd still have plenty of time left."

Over dinner, I felt a rush of guilty concern for this little boy so determined to get on his mother's calendar that he'd already penciled in her objections. He went on to explain that he'd decided that what I should do was make every other Wednesday night a kid-date night. "I don't just mean for me," Danny pointed out. "We could take turns."

That statement replaced my guilty concern with admiration. Was it natural selection, evolutionary skills adapted for survival in our family? His nature? Example? For whatever reason, Danny knows, at eight, something people often spend forty years and thousands of dollars in counseling to learn. He asks for what he needs.

He doesn't demand attention through anger or guilt trips or tantrums (unlike plenty of adults I know). He asks for what he needs. Even if he never develops a degree beyond today, he already has most of the personality skills he'll need. This embryonic man of the twenty-first century has a chance to grow up without a lot of the emotional hangnails boys even of his dad's generation had to accept as part of the package of being male.

By asking me for a date, he also reminded me that this raising-children business isn't just a teaching process. It's a learning process, too. And, though I hate to brag, I also have to think this boy of mine will make a catch for all those twenty-first-century Caitlins and Julias growing up out there. In the year 2005 or so, the line will form on the left.

But I hope Danny sets aside a Wednesday night, every once in a while, for me.

Home-
fires

In a Heartbeat,
New Life

NOT long ago, my husband, Dan, set out on what would be the most difficult journey of his adult life.

It would be harder, even, than the trip he made to Chicago twelve years ago for the funeral of his younger brother Fred, killed by a drunken driver. This time, Dan was on his way to see his other younger brother, Rich, who lived in Florida and who was dying of heart disease.

With all of his heart, Dan hoped that his brother, barely forty, would live even another year. In his rational mind, which tends to proceed along pretty pragmatic lines, he knew that in all likelihood he never would see Rich again.

Dan knew all of the things he wanted to say, except for one. He didn't know what he would say when his week's vacation was over, and it was time to hug his brother and say good-bye.

Rich was not even thirty-five when he had his first major heart attack. It was followed, several years later, by another one. And doctors told my brother-in-law in clear language that, in order to cling to life at all, he had to give up his companion of twenty years—Marlboros—and change his life utterly.

He tried. But it was too late. By spring, a doctor at the Cleveland Clinic told Rich that his heart literally was coming apart. There was no alternative but a heart transplant; but again, it probably was too late.

Finally, a couple of weeks before Dan's trip, Rich entered Tampa General Hospital in miserable shape, on the top of the A-list of candidates for a new heart. But because donors are scarce and waiting lists average several months, it seemed fairly clear that Rich had run out of luck.

But on Dan's third night in Florida, he called home, nearly inarticulate with excitement. Astonishingly, a donor had become available; the family, now gathered, was awaiting tests to see if Rich was a "match." At dinner, a call came. The operation was a "go."

By 3 A.M., the new heart beat in my brother-in-law's chest. By midmorning—this part still gives me shivers—his color and general condition were better than they had been in five years.

As the family spokesman, Dan was asked to write to that other family, and the words, even for a veteran reporter, came hard. None seemed large enough. He settled for the simplest, most heartfelt thank-you he could muster. Every day in his thoughts, he said, he repeats it.

We have looked around us, at our family, in recent weeks, with a certain wonderment. Of our four children, two would not be alive except for techniques that didn't exist when my mother was a girl.

One needed extensive blood therapy at birth; another, our youngest, lives in spite of stupefying odds against his birth only because of the scientific artistry of a Milwaukee physician, Paul Katayama, an infertility specialist at Sinai Samaritan Medical Center.

My own brother and his wife, after six miscarriages, found a doctor who diagnosed a rare, difficult immunity problem and, after an intricate course of treatment, they are three-quarters of the way through a normal pregnancy.

Of course, the posture of eternal gratitude is not easy to maintain, and there are plenty of hours when all of us take life for granted, when we moan about money, general woes, each other. But the awareness that we, the most ordinary of families, have been formed and maintained, in real ways, by an age of miracles, never is far away.

My husband and I used to pride ourselves on our wry cynicism, on our edges we kept hard by design. But recent events have chipped those edges.

Hope has exposed our flanks. It is an odd way to feel, and a good one.

When I Lost My Security Blanket

WE were heading north from Green Bay on a recent vacation trip when we heard the muffled cries from the back seat. Our seven-year-old, Bobby, carefully packed into a borrowed station wagon, had become buried under five people and seven days' worth of luggage.

Pulling onto a side road, we rescued our son from the avalanche and, with the help of a few ropes, rearranged the luggage on top of the car. Twenty miles later, I reached for the baby blanket to help soothe our fussy toddler, Martin.

It was gone.

"I saw it with the stuff on top of the car. Don't tell me you didn't put it back in!"

"I thought *you* put it in!"

Another side road. Another scramble under the seats. No blanket. Back twenty miles. A search through a factory field full of old pieces of drywall. Martin, in acute blanket anxiety, cried harder.

It was a windy day, and we had no idea where the blanket had flown off. We drove along the shoulders, looking for a flash of white in the brambles. No luck. One of Martin's big brothers donated his own "blankie" temporarily, and Martin was soothed.

But I wasn't. That puffy little crib quilt was special, passed down through three brothers, washed to a comforting consistency. Its pattern of red and blue birds and brown teddies matched the sheets, and the pattern wasn't made anymore.

My poor little kid, I thought. At sixteen months old, he'll

never even remember this quilt, which, for him, was the surrogate of my arms. But he'll know the loss.

That crib quilt preyed on my mind, and by the time we got to Peshtigo, I was a furious sulk. I'd hurried to save a couple of seconds and regretted it. Life is all seconds, I thought, an unguarded second, a loss, plenty of time to stew.

The Peshtigo Fire Museum used to be a church, and next to the church is a churchyard filled with graves. Like most people who didn't grow up in Wisconsin, I'd never heard of the Peshtigo fire. The worst disaster of its kind in history, the great fire came roaring out of the forests on the very same day, October 8, 1871, and very nearly at the same hour as the great Chicago fire consumed most of that city's core.

The Chicago fire got all of the publicity. Nearly $196 million in damage was recorded, and about 250 people died. But in Peshtigo and the surrounding areas, some 1,200 people died. Only the 1889 Johnstown flood in Pennsylvania took more lives.

We walked out into the churchyard. One tombstone bore the names of the McGregors: parents Sarah and Donald, and Janet, aged 15; Lily, aged 2; Alvey, aged 1. October 8, 1871.

My children ran among the stones. Martin rolled around on the warm grass. I picked him up and he struggled, sweet-smelling and strong. I had lost his blanket, a piece of cloth, and spent hours fussing over it.

I set Martin down and he rubbed his fingers on the soapy white stone. Lily, aged 2. Alvey, aged 1.

We wandered through the museum, which is filled with photos and relics of the fire. The museum, which I had visited before, is a quiet place. We looked at a can of berries, charred to fossil. Paging through a pamphlet, I came upon the eyewitness account of the Reverend Peter Pernin, who wrote of citizens rushing through the darkness and the keening wind to the banks of the Menominee River.

One was a mother, carrying her child wrapped in a blanket. As Pernin watched, she glanced down and discovered that her baby was not among the blankets. Pernin tried to comfort her, "but she stood there motionless, her eyes wild and staring." She had fled in terrible haste. Another second. All she held in her arms was a blanket.

A Cheesehead Lament

I read a story the other day about how scorn for fat people is the last acceptable prejudice. You wouldn't dare to slam a person's race or age or handicap or affectional preference. But it's still all right to say overweight people are sloppy.

Actually, the story didn't quite go far enough.

There is one other acceptable prejudice, and since I do the majority of my business with people outside our fair state, I have an intimate acquaintance with it.

It's Wis-Dain. Prejudice against people from Wisconsin.

Actually, most people I encounter don't consider Wisconsin natives chunky of both wit and limb—but only because they don't really know where Wisconsin is. To coastals, Wisconsin is part of the Great Out There, a little to the left of North Dakota, a place you don't have to know about unless you're running for president.

"So how are things in Michigan?" an editor at one of the magazines to which I contribute stories used to ask me whenever I called. The first time, I told him gently, "I don't know how things are in Michigan. I'm in Wisconsin."

The next few times, I didn't bother to say anything because I realized that, to this nice guy, I was part of the Mich-Wis-Minn-Iowa void.

I used to like to tell the story about the time I was to appear on the *Donahue* show, and the publicist at my book publisher asked me, ever so kindly, what I planned to wear. Without thinking, I told the truth. "A green suit," I said.

She said softly: "Ah. A green suit."

When I encountered her in the lobby of Rockefeller Plaza, she greeted me with disproportionate joy. I was wearing a raw silk turquoise skirt and jacket, what we in the territories call "a green suit." She told me she had spent a few nail-chewing hours wondering if I'd show up in something with the name of a snowmobile club on the back.

A young woman from a Los Angeles television studio fairly trilled the other day when I identified the source of my area code. "Wisconsin!" she said. "Wow! I bet there's snow there!"

"And ice," I said helpfully.

"And deer," she said.

"Yes," I told her. "One just walked across my yard. I stood out on the porch and shot it."

"Really?" she said and was disappointed when I told her I was fooling. "You think, you know . . . Wisconsin!"

What do you actually think? I wondered. That we all turn our parkas fur side out for formal occasions? That even the women have to wear suspenders to keep our pants over our beer bellies?

Maybe Wisconsin will attain new status now that not one but two of Bill Clinton's cabinet members—Les Aspin and Donna Shalala—hail from here. (Though Shalala isn't really from Wisconsin, she is from Ohio, which is almost the same thing, and she spent five years here.)

I've spent time figuring out the right response to that faint shake of the head that always greets me when I tell people where I'm from. And I think the next time I encounter a New Yorker who snaps a finger and says, "Wisconsin! Cheese, right?" I'm going to point right back and say, "New York! Crime, right?"

The Dark Side
of the Road

WE were coming up over a hill about an hour after sunset when I noticed it—a sort of gap in the motion of the car where the acceleration should have been. Then the car stopped. I coasted for the shoulder. A check under the hood revealed nothing I could jiggle or reconnect.

There we were—my three young sons and I—on a country highway in Wisconsin middle of nowhere, about twenty miles from the nearest place with a name.

We locked the doors. I couldn't leave the children and hike to a farmhouse; and I couldn't risk taking them with me.

My husband didn't expect us home from a weekend visit to Grandpa at any particular time, and in any case he wouldn't worry. He never doubted that I could protect myself and the kids in any fix. Nor did I.

"We'll just turn on the emergency flashers and the police will come," I said to the boys. A half-hour. An hour.

"Will the police come soon?" my three-year-old asked.

"Of course," I told him, with more confidence than I, by then, felt. I was fashioning newspaper headlines in my mind: "Motorists Report Seeing Slain Family on Roadside."

Then I began to think of other stories, of children who drowned in accidents while their parents watched helplessly, of children who died in fires in upstairs rooms while their parents ran out to seek help and lived. I had reacted to those stories with pity, but anger, too. Why had those parents failed?

One of the perks of parenthood, after all, is a sense of power. If you can mold lives, you also can protect them. Yet now I was swamped. I could do nothing. My fear of no one stopping gave way to my fear of who would.

Just then, my nine-year-old popped up out of the back seat. He had fashioned a white flag from his shirt, a rubber band and the tire iron. Leaning out the window, he began to wave it. "Don't worry, Mom," he said. "I saw this on *MacGyver*."

And sure enough, in five minutes a car stopped. Locking the children in, and flipping on the brights (to blind the other motorist), I walked down the road. Ten feet. He was big. Fifteen feet . . . he was Ted Bundy . . . twenty feet . . . he was a kid in a T-shirt looking at the tire iron in my hand with a mixture of alarm and amusement. He went home and called for help.

The boys got a swell ride home in a State Patrol cruiser; I got a ride with a taciturn tow-truck operator. At home, the night sounds outside now comforting, fears rushed in.

I could joke—who says action TV shows aren't educational?—but awful things could have befallen us. Awful things befall parents and children every day, on the road, in their homes, and not because lesser parents have a failure of wit or will.

I'd convinced myself my devotion gave us special protection; I had, in my arrogance, mistaken good luck for capability. I'd forgotten how at the mercy of fate all of us are. That recognition crashed down on me, leaving me bowed, not with fear, but with humility.

That night, before I slept, I thought back to all those stories, all those anguished families caught in a dark place to which deliverance never came. Watching my children curled in their beds, I closed my eyes and asked the forgiveness of all those parents I had wronged, those whose names I remembered and those whose names I'd never known.

How Now, the Vanishing Cow

BRANTWOOD, Wisconsin—We came here, to a farm at the southernmost edge of the North Woods, to stay for a weekend so that our children could touch cows.

We thought it odd that these Wisconsin-raised children still considered cows something you count from the car window. Living in the midst of some of the richest agricultural country in America, they were city kids who knew only from TV the true story about the chicken and the egg.

It's called Palmquist's Farm, and for forty years it's been taking in lodgers. Most have been winter sportsfolk and hunters who traverse the eight hundred acres and chow down on the hearty, Finnish-style country meals. Now, the family is expanding their summer guest operation, to welcome more families.

Part of the reason is that Helen and Jim Palmquist, who have a young daughter—representing the fifth generation of Palmquists to farm this land—love guests, especially families. It's work that is fun. Part of the reason is that their farm's immense beauty is now its most important economic asset.

"Agricultural is hard," Jim Palmquist said simply. "And it's harder up here than most places. The fields are rocky and triangular in shape. It's harder to grow things."

The Palmquists have given up milking sixty dairy cows. Now, they raise heifers for herd replacement, and beef cows, but even that provides only a slender profit. It costs more to run a farm than a farm can make.

Our children didn't really realize they were learning

firsthand about the besieged agricultural base of their home state's economy as they slid down bales in the hay loft or watched a farm hand (a Czech graduate student on an exchange program) blow feed into the silo. But even the littlest ones could feel the warmth of the egg fresh from beneath a hen, and they saw the intimate relationship between the milk taken from Ingrid, the cow, early each morning, and the brimming glasses on the dinner table.

"They give the chickens grain, and the chicken gives them eggs," I told our five-year-old.

"Like trading!" he said. Yes, I said, it's a trade.

It's a trade for the Palmquists, too. They've changed their life on the farm to include others, and they get to keep the land that's been in their family for five generations. They'll keep their independence, too.

This—the independence, the lifestyle they keep with enormous stress and government support—is something people like to cuss. Let those who can't cut it be chained to a desk or a factory or the wheel of a truck like the rest of us. Life is hard; why should we care? The family farm is a sad, old Wisconsin story. Some people are tired of hearing it.

But at the Palmquists' farm at sunset, watching deer graze near the line of dark woods, it seems like a story new all over again. Maybe farms owned by a canning company are more efficient; but they aren't better. Maybe it's sentimental to believe that people like the Palmquists, and others more fully engaged in working farms, should be where they are, even if the rest of us have to live more ordinary lives. But they should.

So long as we can furnish our minds with the images of the family farm, perhaps we won't lose all connection with the life most of our ancestors lived. Life already is too much a big mall and not enough a general store. We should hold on while we can.

Bonfire of
the Insanities

WE are standing here on fifty acres of sculptured prairie, watching an event that has no use and damages air quality.

It's a bonfire.

You think you've seen a bonfire. But I am here to tell you that this is the kind of bonfire that makes you believe that any minute people in wolf skins will show up with straw manikins and bags of frog parts.

It's October, and the flames of this bonfire shoot fifty feet into the air. The pile of brush and wood is twenty feet high and fully that wide. It's been burning three hours. Now they're trying to settle it down.

What this is, is a fund-raiser for a venerable organization called Open Lands, a land-preservation group. There have been clowns and a petting zoo and a ninety-piece bagpipe orchestra. Hours ago.

Those of us left standing here, after all the lawyers and doctors and husbands of lawyers and doctors and others have cleared off, are a motley group. Two businessmen with pitchforks, wearing bow ties and eagerly tending the dying blaze. Two firefighters about twenty years old. A percussionist. Two dancers. A painter. A novelist. And me.

We are talking about neither art nor fund-raising. All we can talk about is the fire. It fills our eyes, bisects us into a hot front panel and a shivering back end, because it's late at night. It makes us talk about funny things.

"Sometimes," says the novelist, "when I stand on the subway platform, I just have this wish; it's not to die, but to just fall."

"Don't you have it now? Don't you want to see what it would be like to walk into the fire?" asks the painter.

"Buildings," says one of the dancers. "High buildings or mountains. It's so strong you almost have to consciously remind yourself not to go to the edge and try it."

"It mesmerizes you, no doubt about it," says one of the young firefighters. "Once, my helmet melted, but I was concentrating so hard on the fire I didn't notice. I smelled the steam off it. My cheeks were raw."

The sparks fly up, into a wavering wall of heat. The fire looks like a pile of autumn leaves, that very same motion, only each leaf is a separate orange billow—or a garden, a mound of blossoms, all alight.

All at once, we say the same thing: What is it about this? What would we do without fire?

"You need it," says the painter. "Human beings do. You need wood fires."

Someone else points out that, of course, we don't need it at all. We don't need it, most of us, for warmth or to cook.

"No, of course," says the painter. "What you need is the smell. You need . . . the proof."

The proof probably is different for each of us. For the firefighters and the businessmen in their bow ties (probably more for the businessmen), the fire is a manly right. They're jockeying to mess with the two-inch hose hooked to a portable water tank, wading into the fire in rubber boots, standing in it, experiencing, for a moment, that jump off the subway platform.

For others of us, it's probably evidence that we can hold off the night, some memory older than race—a reminder that the same element that could consume us also protects.

Still others think of moon religions, of what drew people out of the villages, onto the hillsides in the nights of fall. We feel close to something wild, which has nothing to do with TV.

We are fascinated, returned to children. When a hot spot

shoots a blue jet of flame up for a moment, I literally have to remind myself to close my mouth.

We are watching a sort of celebration of air pollution. A minor mess. A potential threat. One of the most gorgeous things I've ever seen.

It will burn until morning and return in dreams.

A Quiet Place,
and Green

ONE drizzly afternoon in Chicago, I took my sons and one of their friends to some quintessential attractions.

In suburban Forest Park, there are more dead people than living. Mike Todd, Elizabeth Taylor's second or third or whatever husband, is buried in Waldheim Jewish Cemetery. Up the road, Alphonse Capone lies in Hillside.

I like cemeteries, everything about them. My grandfather and I would go for strolls in cemeteries when I was a little girl, and sit on the cold marble slabs of the stones on hot days.

The epitaphs were my first literature—poignant and powerful and much to the point. They were the great lyric of a grieving lover's life, much of the time. A parent. A husband. A best friend.

I showed the boys one of my favorites: DEATH BE NO PROUD, it says.

The quotation wasn't worn away by time; it's never been correct. There's no name, only dates, so I've always wondered: Was the writer non-English-speaking, the customer the same? But readers both, proud of a single, bold sentiment?

We ambled to Showman's Rest, a very peculiar spot near the front gates of Woodlawn Cemetery, off Division Street. Two large monuments in the shape of gray circus elephants mark the plot.

As best as I can determine from all the stories I've heard and sketchy accounts I've read, this is the resting place of circus folk, most of them from a train that burned in Chicago in 1915. Urban legend has it that the charred remains of the elephants are buried there as well; I doubt this, but would rather go on believing that the bones of giants slumber beneath my feet when I walk here.

Wandering along the rows, we gazed at graves eloquent in their very lack of identification. "Unknown Male No. 20." "Unknown Male No. 26." Lines of them. And named people, too, one called "Shorty." "A midget?" asked my seven-year-old. One called "Irish." One called "Ma." I speculated aloud about all those unknowns. Circus performers, I guess, then and now—probably more then—are restless people. Could they have vanished so thoroughly from wherever they were born that even eight decades in the future no one had come to claim Billy or Sam or Moe?

Some of the graves were newer, as well, only a few years old, leading me to believe that this was still a place where performers took their rest, just as the cemetery in Paris I dragged my oldest son to see seemed to have a premium on poets and their sweethearts.

"Now," I said with motherly efficiency as we got back into the car, "wasn't that interesting?" The older boys nodded silently, but my four-year-old grew angry.

"Interesting?" he said. "How can you say all those people dying that long ago was interesting? It's sad, Mom. It's real sad."

I felt abashed. He knows what he's talking about. He's seen death in all its silence and sorrow, before the peace of a cemetery cloaks it in grass and in grace. The squirrel in the pool. The neighbor's dog. His father.

I still like cemeteries. But I respect my son's need to temper my wish to pay attention to the words on the stones with his wish to pay respect to the purpose for them.

The Place
Where Magic Lives

WHEN we were newlyweds, the first place my husband and I went camping together was a campground on the Chippewa Indian Reservation in Lac du Flambeau. One of the first things we did was row our boat across the short distance to Strawberry Island.

"This is a magical place," said my husband, who'd been going to Lac du Flambeau for ten years before we ever moved to Wisconsin. "It's said to be the site of the final battle between the Chippewa and the Sioux three hundred years ago."

After that legendary conflict, the Sioux were expelled from Wisconsin, and the island became sacred ground to the Chippewa.

At the time, I figured, Well, the guy's in love. It looks like a nice enough place and all, but magical?

However, as the years went by, some of the most magical times we ever spent as a family were around the shores of Strawberry Island. We taught our oldest son and our daughter to swim in the little white-sand shoals off the island. We fished there, and ate picnic lunches on the shore. We learned, from the Indians we met around town, that the island contains the bones of ancestors more than two thousand years old.

For eighteen years, every summer, we spent part of our vacation exploring the island, never taking anything away, never touching anything in a way meant to harm, simply visiting.

And, after a while, I came to agree. It was a magical place.

My grandmother was an Indian, a Cree, and though she

lived most of her life in a white world, she often told me that places are imbued with their histories, and that no amount of change could remove that spirit or violate it.

We'll see.

Strawberry Island is now part of a confusing deal, involving state and federal officials, to swap the island for federally owned land in Aspen, Colorado. A few weeks ago, an Aspen developer received a building permit to construct a vacation house on the island—named last year by the State Historical Society as one of the state's most endangered historic places.

The developer, a man named Walter Mills, offered the swap, three acres of federal land for sale in Aspen in exchange for the twenty-six acres of Strawberry Island.

If that sounds like the kind of deal Indians have gotten used to over the past couple of hundred years of U.S. history, that's probably not much of an understatement.

There's confusion over the jurisdiction of the land, which was given to the tribe in 1854 under a treaty agreement, but allotted in parcels to individuals under the Davies Allotment Act of 1887. Most Chippewa apparently believed the land still belonged to the tribe as a whole, until workers authorized by individual tribal members began cutting down trees and marking off plots in 1993.

Not long ago Madison lawyer Carol Brown Biermeier, a Lac du Flambeau Chippewa, began negotiating for a return of the land to the tribe, trying to save a small space that probably hasn't much significance for many people, but probably a great deal of significance for a few.

In the end, the action succeeded. It wasn't just good luck. It was good medicine.

You can suggest that a vacation home wouldn't have much effect on a whole island. Not every lovely place on earth needs to be pristine. But what it would do is blur the edges between

Strawberry Island and the rest of the world, just as the vigorous development of much reservation land has driven a wedge between the space and its past.

When that happens, a spirit, no matter how deep its roots, might have a hard time clinging. I'm not a Chippewa, but even for me, that would be a tragedy.

The last time I visited Strawberry Island, a dozen of my family members and I cruised its shores in a boat one summer afternoon a few weeks after my husband died in June 1993. In a small brown envelope, we carried a tiny handful of his ashes, which we scattered in those white-sand shallows. As we did—and you will think this is wishful fiction, but I have witnesses—two eagles dipped low over the water and crossed paths.

And what had been a place of restful joy became a resting place—for Dan and for scores of other souls before him. A place that belongs to history, to visit but not to plunder. A place that should not need a sign that says, DO NOT DISTURB.

Natural
Causes

The Mother of My Child

MOTHER'S Day is not the only time I think of her, but it's the only time I can't avoid it. She was going to have a child but couldn't keep it. I wanted a child desperately but couldn't have one. She was the mother at birth; I was the mother right after. It sounded simple, but it wasn't.

In the beginning, she was just a voice on the telephone from 150 miles away. She was the one who answered my ad in an alternative newspaper—one of those notices you see that begins, "Loving couple, in their thirties, unable to bear children . . ." From that first moment, I liked everything about her, and that impression never wavered as we progressed from businesslike strangers exchanging résumés to intimates planning a tender offer of the heart.

For more than five months, we talked almost daily on the phone, each of us hungry to learn everything about the other. I tried to picture Amy in my mind's eye, playing with the few details I knew—auburn hair, 120 pounds, five feet four— like a child toying with different configurations of blocks. I imagined her smile, the clothes she wore, the bird feeder in her yard. It helped make her real. It helped me to trust her. And she seemed to need the same kind of details from me. "Describe the new slipcovers," she would say. "Tell me all about the dog."

Night after night, I would run in the door, drop my purse on the floor, and call Amy. Sometimes she'd beat me to it; her voice would be waiting for me behind the blinking red light on the answering machine. "Hi, babe," she'd greet me. "Guess what?" The social worker had sent her forms, she'd say. The ultrasound showed a whopping, thriving fetus. At times we wouldn't even mention the legal plans and details that would attend my adoption of the baby growing inside her.

Amy sounded like every girl I grew up with in Chicago—bighearted, wisecracking, mostly uneducated, but possessed of a fierce, intuitive set of smarts. Her slang, her very accent, comforted me.

Often I would hear her six-year-old son, from her former marriage, playing happily in the background. So she was a good mother. That was nice. Or was it? Could a good mother, who knew what it was to love a child, give up a baby? I couldn't see how.

The summer shadows deepened in the corners of the yard. The baby was two weeks late. Then on August 9, 1986, there was no answer when I called. Not the first time, not the second or fifth or tenth. There was no question about it; Amy had to be in the hospital. And I had to hear her voice telling me she hadn't changed her mind. Because that was always a possibility.

Amy was twenty-six, no panicky teenager. She was divorced, poor, but part of a big, proud, urban Irish family. Daily, she had told me, her mother pressured her to keep the baby. But Amy was steadfast. She could raise one alone. Not two. That's what she had said during the long months of her pregnancy. Would she still feel that way now?

Finally, just before 4 P.M., I pressed the redial on the phone and an unfamiliar woman's voice answered. "Who is this, please?" she asked sharply.

"I'm, ah . . . I'm the lady from Wisconsin," I said. "Has Amy said anything about me?"

There was a pause before the voice said coolly, "I'm Amy's sister. You're the lady who was going to adopt the baby. Amy had the baby today. A little boy."

A boy. All my visions of pinafores and teeny tights melted away into an image of a big, sturdy, dark-haired son. But . . . maybe not.

"Did Amy intend . . . did she say she had changed her plans?"

"She said nothing about it," her sister replied, and then her voice softened. "I know this must be hard for you, but I just don't know."

And for two days there was no knowing. I called again and spoke with Amy's mother, who said that her daughter was struggling with what was suddenly a very difficult decision, and would I do her the kindness of letting her make it without my influence? I promised that I would.

But on the evening of the third day, after I had clawed rows of welts along my forearms, I could wait no longer. I called the hospital, and they connected me with Amy's room.

I told her who I was. There was a long silence. Then, weak and sounding far away, she said, "Hi, babe."

She was terribly ill. She had suffered through an emergency cesarean. She had pneumonia. Her mother had talked the nuns into placing her in isolation; by rights, my phone call should not even have been put through. I made small noises of concern. But finally I had to ask.

"Amy, have you changed you mind? If you have I'll hang up and wish you well and you'll never hear from me again. If you tell me to go ahead, I'll set things in motion."

She paused so long that I thought she had dropped the phone. Then she said, "Go ahead."

I made a big okay sign to my husband, who stood nearby, supporting himself on the kitchen counter. "But there's one thing," Amy said. "I want to see you."

We had never discussed this possibility. I didn't know how I felt about it. Once I put a face—a real face, not the smiling, benevolent visage I had concocted in my mind—to that familiar voice, would it haunt me for the rest of my life? Would I see it every time I looked at the child I already knew would be called Daniel Chamberlain—after his father, Dan, and his father's historical hero, Joshua Chamberlain, one of the heroes of the Battle of Gettysburg?

But I pushed my doubts aside. There was nothing I wouldn't do to bring Daniel home.

Twenty hours later, my husband and I were in a crowded Chicago hospital, picking our way nervously down corridors to the maternity floor, expecting to be stopped at any moment. The nun gave me a measuring look when I asked for Amy. She was still in isolation and no one but close family was allowed in the room when the baby was present. But as I learned later from a hospital social worker, the nun knew exactly who we were and decided to let God work it out.

She showed us to a cramped little room. Amy was sitting on the bed in a blue peignoir set that would have been right at home in an old Doris Day movie. Her hair was brick red; I knew right away that she had called it auburn to sound more sophisticated. She looked up. She was a pretty woman, with freckles and a generous mouth and the oddest-color eyes— neither brown nor hazel but like a leaf just beginning to turn in the fall.

"Jack?" she said, using the nickname I had heard so often on the phone. My throat was too full for me to do anything but nod.

She stood up and came into my arms. We held each other silently. My husband put his arms around us both.

Then she turned to the Plexiglas bassinet that had been partially hidden behind her. She reached in and picked up a baby as big and bonny and rosy dark as I had imagined him. "Look, Danny," she said. "I told you Mommy and Daddy were coming."

My husband made a sound somewhere between a cough and a sob. Amy placed Danny in my arms.

As I nuzzled the baby, she crowed over him like any proud mother. "Isn't he beautiful?" she said. "See how big he is? See? He knows it's you. He smiled."

I was lost in him. The bonds radiated from him and locked me fast. What could I say? How could I compliment her on the fine son she had borne? Facing me was the mother who had suffered a massive physical assault to give him life. A woman who had turned her back on her family's offers of help and her obstetrician's referral to a wealthy North Shore couple who could give this boy things we never could. Amy had not broken our trust. I appreciated that then. I'm awestruck by it now.

Amy and I traded Danny back and forth. Then his new father held him. "Oh, thank you," Dan said over and over. "Thank you. Thank you." It sounded like a prayer.

After a long time, a nurse poked her head in the room. "No one but Mom is supposed to hold the baby," she said gently.

"But I—" I began, and stopped. Amy and I exchanged glances. I returned the baby to his bed. Amy covered him with a doll-size quilt. And then, straightening her shoulders, she began loading my arms with formula and diapers and little plastic containers of powder—all the free gifts that suppliers offer to maternity patients.

"I won't need these," she said firmly. "*You* will."

"Wish I could tell you . . ." I said.

Amy stopped me gracefully. "It's okay. I know."

It was over. There would be no more giggling on the telephone. No more trading of the details and secrets of our lives. Danny would be released to the social worker tomorrow; we would bring him home the same day. I would be a new mother.

Dan and I staggered to the elevator and through the lobby without a word. In the parking lot, he leaned against our van, his forearm over his eyes. I have heard him cry before and since, but not this way, not with such great gulps of love and pity. He could think of nothing, he finally said, but of Amy going home alone tomorrow and of some lines from a poem by Stephen Vincent Benét, in which the ghost of Abraham Lincoln's mother asks: "What's happened to Abe? . . . Did he grow tall? . . . Did he get on?"

"How can she bear it?" he said. I told him I didn't know.

We brought Danny home at noon the following day. I had promised Amy a last phone call to let her know we had arrived safely. While the relatives made much of our new addition, I slipped away and called her. She answered on the first ring.

"It's me," I said.

"I knew it would be."

"Are you okay?"

"I'm as well as I can be."

Just before we hung up, she said, "I want you to promise to raise him to be like us. To be tough. Don't let his daddy spoil him." And she added, "I'm glad he's a little boy."

"Why?" I asked.

"Because the world's too tough on little girls," she said.

Except for a single phone call that came a year later on Christmas Day, I have not heard from Amy again. Danny's grown into a bold and tender boy, uniquely at home with the world. He doesn't really look like the fading picture of Amy I keep in my mind—except for his eyes, which are the oddest color, like a leaf just beginning to turn in the fall.

One day, when he can understand, I'll tell my Danny the story of his birth. And if, when he's old enough, he wants to look up the woman who bore him, I will not protest—how could I ever fear Amy? I will ask only one thing: that I be allowed to go with him.

For I have things to tell her. I want her to know that, lo and behold, a couple of months ago the undreamed-of happened and I was able to give Danny a baby brother from my own body. I want to tell her that it was no different, that I love the child I bore no more than the one she placed in my arms. They are both angels of the outside chance.

And there's something else. See, I miss her. I want to know that the world hasn't been too tough on her.

When I do talk to Danny about Amy, I won't know exactly how to describe her. We weren't friends, precisely, nor were we family. It was as if we were strangers who met on a stranded bus and then went our own ways, but not without looking backward, each straining to see where the other was headed.

This much I will be able to tell Danny for certain: that he is who he is not only because he was raised by parents who searched for him and fought for him and adored him, but because of something else, too.

He comes of good stock.

The Last
First Birthday

I phone the pediatrician's receptionist for an appointment for a one-year-old checkup.

"For Martin," I tell her.

"Already?" she asks.

"Already," I say with a sigh.

This confirms it momentarily. It's not only me. This baby's first year really has seemed like a moment.

When I put down that phone, I realize that she probably says this to all of the mothers. Yet, even for us, who see him daily, this child's progress from lap dweller to stair climber has seemed particularly brisk. Last week—two weeks ago at the outside—I was watching *thirtysomething* between contractions, and now when I offer beets to the result of those contractions, he shakes his head and says quite clearly, "No."

I'm not good at this. I'm good at crises. Bring me a cut and I will stanch the bleeding; bring me a tangled schedule and I will sort it out. But I'm not good at good-byes, and a first birthday is a kind of good-bye, a good-bye to infancy—of this baby in particular and, for me, of babies of my own in general.

Busyness is my usual cure. So I sort out the best baby clothes for sisters-in-law, put away the cradle, and pick out crib toys that aren't too fatigued for a garage sale in the spring.

And yet how much this costs me. Every act of closure exacts a toll out of proportion to the effort. It isn't that I wish we could have another—not exactly.

There's barely enough time, enough money, enough of us, the parents, to go around as it is. It isn't so much wanting another as wanting this one back. Wanting back the ordinary instants that I, pulled by six or eight different urgencies, honestly didn't have time to savor.

There are friends of mine who think I'm nutty. They are better at it, at moving along matter-of-factly through ages and stages, bidding cheerful farewells to the clutter of diapers, removing the safety locks from the kitchen cabinets with relief.

And not long ago, I swallowed tears when I talked with an author who'd written a beautiful, funny short story about a baby girl. I thought it was fiction based on life, but she told me she'd never had a baby.

But she'd craved a baby. "That story," she said, "was an attempt to correct life."

To my baby, especially, this all would seem absurd. He's lifting his chin with pride as he manages to stoop and pick up a toy without sitting down. He's fascinated by the fact that making a sound, "Mama," has the effect of bringing me to his side.

We fill up rolls of videotape and film to capture him in all of his comedy, but it doesn't suffice. Even a few months later, time has done its sleight of hand. I can't remember the feel or form or essence of that baby in the clown costume at Halloween. Mondays and holidays and first teeth have whipped past me, the way telephone poles used to whip past the windows of the car when I was a child.

I wonder how much of this is a matter of putting behind me a part of life—call it youth—that once seemed limitless. I wonder if I am nervous about the uncharted territories we are beginning to track with our oldest, who's already a teenager. I think it is less the fear of growing older than it is a simple yearning for more recognition of life before life becomes history.

As Thornton Wilder wrote more than half a century ago, human beings never see life while they live it.

They do, of course. After a brush with tragedy, ordinary life—a cup of tea, the way street lights look through snow—all seems miraculous. And then, because you can't live peeled back with wonder, things settle down.

It doesn't always take a near miss, though, to bring life up close and bring me up short. This birthday, this last first birthday, did that, too.

Trusting the Kindness of Strangers

IT was storming—lightning, thunder, sleet, the whole grim late-autumn bit. One of my sons noticed him first, a little kid, alone, walking down the street, soaked by the elements and crying hard. My son ran to get me. What else could he do?

Of course, within seconds, my children's caregiver and I were all over that kid.

"Honey, did someone hurt you? Are you frightened? Don't you know your way home?"

After a moment, he sobbed, "I'm scared of the thunder."

It took us a few more minutes—by now we were under the roof of the porch—to find out his name was Chris and that he couldn't find the school friend whose house he was supposed to visit, so he was trying to get home.

"How far is home?"

"From my school to my apartment up there, one mile."

He'd come no more than a couple of blocks. The adults exchanged looks over his head as we stood there, debating, in the cold.

Here was a nine-year-old on a cold street. Here was a house warm and bright. Everything we were cried out to us to bring him in, dry him off, and phone his mother. And yet we hesitated.

You don't bring a kid into your home. You don't bring a kid into your home because it confounds all the messages that mothers (this child's probably no exception) try to teach—about strange houses and people who seem as though they want to help and say they'll call mom.

As we trooped inside to find the phone book, my son looked at me piercingly. "Are you going to let him stand out there?" he said. The wind was moaning. I looked at my son.

"Of course not. Chris, come inside. It's okay."

Of course, his mother's number wasn't in the book. And so we faced another dilemma. Did we do what every instinct instructed—and every lesson forbade—and drive him? Or did we send him back down that street, soaked and scared?

We drove him. And on the way we spotted his friend, just a few feet from Chris's house. As he left, we told him he shouldn't take a ride from just anyone, that we were good grown-ups.

But if we'd been bad adults, wouldn't we have said just the same things? And wouldn't this child (or mine or yours) have believed us, in spite of the repeated cautions, the assurances that all bad people don't look the part?

Now there was a kid, home safe because of us. And there was a worry. When he told his mother about the people who drove him home, would her heart contract with fear for an instant?

Would she think how all the new lessons (the stranger-danger ones) didn't match all the old ones: the Good Samaritan ones, the do-unto-others ones? If my child were in the same straits, wouldn't I want Chris's parent or some parent to open the door to him, care for him, save him?

Of course, I would. I think.

The Truth About
That Perfect Shot

THEY looked so beautiful when I pulled the picture out of the envelope that it almost brought me to tears.

Our four children in their Sunday-best-best clothes were seated together, looking off, as if amused, into the middle distance. The two oldest had their heads inclined together as if they'd just shared a secret. The four-year-old looked dreamy, which is just how he is. The littlest looked funny and full of vinegar, which is how he is, too.

Only I knew that that same little two-year-old had just concluded a monumental bellow, that the lovely older daughter had just told me to go run my head under the faucet, that the middle boy had consented to sit still for the picture at all only under the threat of having his light sword taken away forever and, as I heard someone add (could it have been me?), "broken into little pieces."

I don't know a single family portrait that doesn't have a lie beneath it.

The hour before this serene pose was captured on film was a period of stress almost unique in the history of our family. Do children roll on the floor and pop off buttons routinely, or did they do this specially to torment their best clothes—and me?

At length, when I could stand the strain no longer, I decided to go upstairs and sit still until we left for the portrait studio. In a moment, the children all went quiet.

What ailed them? Their father had given each of the three younger ones a big cup of Welch's grape juice. I didn't dare scream for fear that the sound would cause one to spill, but I crept toward them with my knuckles stuffed in my mouth.

In the photo, these children look as though they never fight and call each other "dead meat," as though they never tell each other to look at the spider on the wall in order to grab french fries from each other's plates. They look smooth and good (they are good) like the children in Madeleine L'Engle's old books—like children who say witty, sensitive things at the dinner table, while everyone laughs gratefully.

In fact, my children do laugh a great deal. They laughed when the two-year-old, painstakingly dressed in lawn and linen, plunged his arms into the toilet up to the elbows just before we all piled into the car. (Alternate outfit; much muttering with heads in hands.)

They laughed when their father had to pin my arms behind my back as I attempted one last rush with a comb at the seven-year-old's cowlick.

There's a good reason why I'm not in the picture. By the time we arrived at the photo studio, I looked as though I had crawled a mile on my knees. I was sweating. My hair was pushed up on my head into spikes, and not the fashionable kind either. Delivering these children to the studio in good shape had undone me. I didn't look like the mother of these children. I looked like someone who needed medication to ride in a car.

Was it really worth it to have told our daughter that I would rap her on the head with a brush if she shut her eyes just one more time when the shutter clicked?

Was it worth it to have held the toddler on my lap (to keep him from getting mussed) so tightly he finally tried to bite me?

Was it worth it, this artificially crafted, carefully constructed memory? Wouldn't a snapshot of everyone in sweatpants out at the knees, with makeshift Ninja bands around some of their heads, with the fifteen-year-old in her Andre Agassi T-shirt, size Triple X-Large, done just as well?

Was it worth it? You should see this picture. If this is the way I want to remember this period of life, you can hardly blame me. After all, I paid the price.

One Carpool,
Minus One Mom

I was expelled from the car pool the other day.

It wasn't unexpected: I'd been on waivers since the time I was twenty minutes late after school. But it still sent a sliver into the little space under my heart—the place where I keep proof that ours is just the same as every other family in our neighborhood.

There are a lot of slivers in that place, mostly healed. A school counselor calling me an ambitious career woman not counting the costs to her family. A coworker telling me, at a shower, "At this point, I'm just glad to have a happy husband and healthy children. Other women have bigger concerns. But that's mine."

"It's not your fault," said my seventh grader, after I told him that our carpool now consisted of him, me, and our car. "I could help you."

"It is my fault," I told him. "I'm the mother."

Now, I'm not nailing up a cross for myself here. But my failure to line up the ducks despite two assistants, a sitter, eight phones, five calendars, and a date book, is neither comprehensible nor new: I hear the exasperation in the voice at the dentist's office, the piano teacher, the troop meeting. . . . Right, sure! We didn't forget. Or if we did, I'm sorry. I'm so sorry.

Knowing the nature of the day ahead—visitors from out of town and three kids home, many opportunities for error—other mothers would have done more organizing on the night before, instead of letting even the one-year-old sit up, selfishly, and watch *Party of Five*, just so as to have someone to talk it over with. Other mothers might have begged a friend to stand in or switched days, admitting they could not perform just as ably solo instead of tandem.

Morning, then, would not have come up like thunder. Lost lunches, lost gloves, lost tempers. Change the baby now, or just throw her in her snowsuit? Ferret's loose! The guy from the package express wants you.

I can do this. It's just one week each month.

But not anymore. I don't blame the other parents. My chronic lateness was annoying, even scary. They don't blame me. The four other families are made up of two parents and two children, and two-on-two works better than zone defense, one mom told me. But I'm no poster child for the afflictions of single motherhood. I get to work at home, in my own business. I have help. Given that, it's hard to see how you could still be stretched nearly transparent, from having so much ground to cover.

Before I was widowed, I couldn't see it as well. When divorced moms Leah or Ellen or Lynn showed up late, trailing soccer clothes fresh from the dirty-laundry hamper, I would think, these sisters need to set better priorities.

There are only so many things one person can do.

But what a working single mother has to do is work and be single. Some time ago, stories about Mia Farrow's autobiography told of her legendary tribe of fourteen, seven still at home. Anyone could do it with live-in nannies, people said. But in my experience, when the buck stops—trouble at school, medication lost—it stops with a child's parent, because the parent, whatever else she does, is the one who needs to know.

When single mothers who work take out all the costs and count them, usually about 1 A.M., we find that money or help can only prop a structure that has significant design flaws. A neighbor whose work project was canceled last week said that she spent the day baking cookies with her four-year-old.

Stolen time, she called it: I steal it at bedtime, tacking on more of a day than I should because it's the only day I have.

Now I could have asked the other car poolers, nice people, Please, just help me out for a few months. Let my kid ride along when you go. I'll make it up to you. I know it looks as though I'm deliberately too busy and unorganized to take care of my own—but I'm not doing any of this on purpose.

I didn't say that, though.

There are only so many things one person can do.

Enter the Cowboy

MY father must have thought we were looting his house, trying to lay hands on the inheritance.

For several weekends over a period of months, my brother and I went deep down into the dusty recesses of forty years' worth of boxes and bags of photos and cards and mementos that my mother and father were collecting long before they ever thought of us.

We were trying to collect enough evidence for a testimonial to our father's life.

Actually, we were trying to come up with a holiday gift for someone who likes only a few things besides his family—golf shoes, Manhattan cocktails, and pea soup—which limits you.

So we decided on the new gift thing—a video made from photo transfers and snippets of old film. Though my friend Susan makes such films with bewitching artistry, she could make the music only if we provided the score.

That wasn't easy. We had to pore over photos we hadn't seen since childhood and try to match faces with names. Our dad is the only surviving member of his generation of relatives. So there was no one to ask for help. We had to try to piece things together like archeologists, from hints—the kinds of clothes people were wearing, the way the faces matched our memories.

We collected all the pictures familiar to us: those that dealt with our own childhoods, our family trips, our own weddings, our father with his grandchildren. We selected curled old Polaroids of our parents working on the symbol of success in their 1960s neighborhood—an apartment over three stores. And we decided to throw in some of my father's "horse pictures."

We knew that, long ago, my father had ridden in rodeos, an era so remote that it had mostly comic significance. We found some of his ribbons, pictures of my mother in her own riding clothes. We didn't know whether the videographer would even want to use them.

But she was enraptured. She'd done this often enough to be able to spot the lyric moment in a life when she saw it. The image of our father, straight in his saddle with the silver trappings, told her, she said, that "this was really the story of a handsome young cowboy in love with a beautiful girl."

We looked at the old photos with new eyes. And we saw it. Not the dad we knew, in grimy work clothes and a work cap, or in loud golf clothes with suspenders hiking up an ample belly, but a hero on a fine horse that he'd lovingly trained, who caught the eye of the women and the respect of the men.

We felt almost presumptuous, intruding on this private image. It had nothing to do with us. And yet everything . . .

We tried our best with the tape. Our father is, after all, our father to us. He cannot be other. But our vicarious journey through his life left us reflecting about who people really are as they age and change. I thought about what my story will be when my children tell it, and how different it might be from the story I'd tell of myself.

Heaven, somebody said once, will be an unusual place because everyone will be thirty years old. I don't know what our father sees in his mirror every morning. But these days I hope that, just as I sometimes see the suntanned high-school senior looking out from behind my bleary eyes, he sometimes sees the cowboy.

Little House of
Life Lessons

I'M midway through my fourth reading of the Laura Ingalls Wilder books, the series of seven pioneer stories that children call the Little House books.

The recipient of the bedtime reading this time around is my
six-year-old son, Danny. Before him, we read them to our older
son, now nine, and to our daughter, now seventeen. That
would only make three readings, but I count my own childhood readings of those stories about Laura and Mary and Ma
and Pa.

My mother read me the first three or so. Then I took over.
It's been the same in our own family. We start out with *Little
House in the Big Woods* (in kindergarten), and by the time we're
up to *By the Shores of Silver Lake*, we're getting to first grade
and starting to be able to read.

When I began reading these books to our daughter, I realized that some of those sentences had become as much part of
my past as my own memories.

There's a controversy now over whether Laura Wilder or
her grown daughter really wrote those books. Does it matter?
What if the stories were the mother's and the sweet, simple
prose was influenced by the daughter? That would not change
the legacy of the books for me—the beliefs about ways of living that I realized have become part of my own value system.

We almost hesitated before we began reading them to our
oldest son. Were these "girl" books? Would he reject them? We
hesitated for about fifteen minutes. From the first page, he fell
in love.

As prairie settlers not long after the Civil War, the Ingalls family was poor. They were as brutally poor as some disadvantaged urban families now. Of course, as a child, I didn't realize that what I was reading was the chronicle of a brute struggle for survival. I thought the plague of grasshoppers and the constant search for better land were part of an enthralling adventure.

But what Laura was writing about, along with sweet memories of a pioneer girlhood, was a hand-to-mouth existence, constantly threatened by the climate, politics, wolves, illness. Laura's older sister, Mary, was blinded by fever. Repeatedly, the family lost the homes they had built with their own hands.

They had only three books. Some winters they would not have had coats except for the charity of wealthy Easterners who sent aid packages. The food they ate through many winters compares almost exactly with modern descriptions of subsistence diets in Third World countries.

Yet they persevered. They did not lose their dignity, even when faced with crushing deprivation and fear. They continued to believe that life, with all its blows, was worth the living.

When my six-year-old, to whom Santa brings trucks and robots and board games, learns that Mary and Laura got only a penny and a few pieces of hard candy in their stockings—and considered that bountiful—he asks, "Didn't Santa have as much money back then?" I don't know how to answer him, except to tell him that, each in our own time, we need to be grateful for what we have, whatever it is we have.

The lives of Laura and her family are a model for grace under pressure. My children wouldn't understand the term, but through these books, they understand how grace behaves— how it shoulders hardship and goes on.

I'm glad I have another child, another cycle through these books ahead of me. Everyone needs to be reminded of the virtue of ordinary courage. Every child. Every parent, too.

Tragedy in a Bottle

ONE of the most chilling memories I have is interviewing the grandmother of a teenager who'd died in a car wreck near the Minnesota border.

It had been a two-car crash: both cars had been filled with drunken and underage teens. A few lived. A few died.

Gingerly, fearful of causing more pain, I broached the subject of drinking, and the grandmother said, "Well, of course, he was only doing what we all did. When my husband was young, we'd drive around with the keg on the floor of the car, too."

I wanted to get up and run. Something inside me had expected this woman to stand up and start screaming: "It stops here! No one in this family ever drinks and drives again!"

Instead, she said essentially, That's life and death in Wisconsin.

Although I can't recall for sure, I don't think I even included that quote in the story I wrote. It was too horrible.

A survey issued by the Department of Public Instruction showed that 52 percent of Wisconsin parents don't object to teens having a drink on a holiday or other special occasion. The State Superintendent said adults should examine their own beliefs about drinking: beliefs that might help explain Wisconsin's losing battle with underage drinking.

Last year, a friend told me about a party her son had attended. The parents served margaritas to the twenty-one-year-olds and the fifteen-year-olds alike. They planned to drive everyone home; they knew the kids would drink anyway. The parents' point of view seemed to be this: Isn't it better to at least supervise kids' partying? At least, if the parents were home, the kids would be supervised, or so the rationale went. They'd learn, at home, the lesson of drinking responsibly.

When I told my teenager this story, she was decidedly unhorrified. "Kids know their parents drink, and parents know kids drink," she said. "At least they weren't hypocrites."

So, by teenager logic, if we shared a backyard beer with our daughter, we'd be hip.

But what worse form of hypocrisy could there be than breaking down the roles as well as the rules between parent and child? Wouldn't we be telling her, Okay, we're peers, but not really? You can drink, but we can drink more? The liquor itself might not harm her. But the message would.

The parents in the Department of Public Instruction survey are right, though. Children can learn responsible drinking at home—by seeing their parents drink, and by talking about drinking responsibly.

Parents want their children to grow up and handle sex responsibly, too. But most wouldn't advocate letting teens practice at home, on special occasions. But teens can learn from their parents' own responsible behavior and attitudes toward sex.

Do we know our seventeen-year-old daughter has experimented with drinking? We know; and she knows we know. But that's not the same as approving or being "understanding." We wouldn't serve her a mixed drink. We aren't going to serve her a mixed message, either.

Just the Truth,
Kids, Not the Facts

MY friends and I ask one another, Would you ever leave your sleeping baby alone in the house for twenty minutes while you ran to the supermarket? Would you fake an excuse for school so your child could go to the circus? Would you give your three-year-old a pacifier?

But none of those is the essay question that counts for a third of your grade: What would you tell your children, we ask one another, about the mistakes of your past—the sex, drugs, alcohol, and other awful things that still make you wince? Would you tell the truth? Would you tell something that resembles the truth? Would you . . . lie?

When I say firmly, without hesitation, that I would lie, some of my friends blanch.

Ours, after all, is the generation that founded its coming of age on a revolt against hypocrisy—and isn't that, after all, what I'm proposing: spin-doctoring my past with the sang-froid of a career politician?

How can you? they say; it's so unlike you.

True, lying to my children would be out of character for me. My kids have seen me drive back across town to pay for the toaster a salesclerk forgot to ring up. And they know I'd have done it even if they weren't in the car.

So I thought long and hard before I could justify certain exceptions to the rule. My decision came gradually, only after I realized that there are several things in life even more important to me than my ideals: the health and safety of my children, and the love and protectiveness I feel for them.

My friend Gary, who has three young sons, could not dis-
agree with me more. He thinks that withholding the truth is
just as bad as telling a lie, and that you never do a child a fa-
vor by lying. "I think my oldest son respects me because I'm
honest. I don't want him to think I'm perfect, because otherwise how is he ever going to learn that people can make mistakes and survive them?" Gary asks me.

Accordingly, Gary, in a discussion about bike helmets, has
told his nine-year-old son, Clay, that he used to ride a motor-
cycle without a helmet—and what a stupid thing that was to
do. When the subject arises years down the road, he'll also tell
his son about the night he spent in jail after he went out drinking with friends, and how, humiliated and sick, he had to face
his mother's disappointment. "Honesty can be hard," he says,
"but hypocrisy can kill you."

Much as I respect Gary, I don't entirely agree. Lucky people
learn from their own mistakes, but they usually don't learn
from other people's, even if those people are the most important figures in their lives.

What children come away with, after the hair-raising de-
tours so many of them seem to take during their teens and
twenties, is their parents' basic values and behavior. As compelling as peer pressure is, of the young people questioned in
a 1991 Roper youth poll, the largest number cited their parents
as their most influential role models.

I don't, however, think that parents should present themselves as paragons. And my husband and I don't. We apologize
to our children when we've lost our tempers. We admit that
we sassed our parents, broke the rules, slapped our younger
brothers. Would I try to keep it from my children that alco-
holism ran like bitter sap through previous generations of our
family tree? No. They have a right, and a need, to know that.

So what, exactly, would I fudge? Those stupid, rash mistakes that could have ruined a life or ended it. Unlike some of

my peers, I haven't completely repudiated those salad days when indulging in casual sex and recreational drugs was a litmus test to prove how antiestablishment we were. I don't think of those practices now as wholly evil or debauched. But neither were they, as people thought then, harmless. Twenty years of history bear witness to the fact that drugs can lay waste to families and whole neighborhoods, and that casual sex can have a lethal undertow.

Not long ago, a young college student in our community, one of those smart, funny young men who seem pointed like an arrow at success, fell to his death from the window of his seventh-story dorm room. His friends said it was only the second time he'd tried LSD. That tragedy strengthened my resolve. I silently vowed to throw all the furniture I could against the door of disaster—with education, role modeling, and long talks—to keep my children safe from such risks. Nor will I allow my own youthful mistakes to provide any possible justification for similar acts on their parts, for I suspect that if I did tell all, my sins might provide more of a rationale than a lesson.

On the day our fourteen-year-old was discovered to have a "friend's" cigarettes in her pocket, she didn't remember all the years I've spent as a nonsmoker; she reached back to the time before I quit: "You smoked! What's the big deal?" That she was just out of grade school and that I'd been in college when I took my first drag didn't matter to her; only that information about me was there, and it hung in the air between us.

After I told my friend Grace about this, she told me an even more harrowing story. When Grace was all of fifteen, she had a full-blown love affair with her twenty-four-year-old gym teacher. Chances are Grace's children aren't going to ask her if she ever slept with a teacher while she was in high school; they may, however, ask about their mom's youthful sexuality in general. What will Grace tell them? Not the truth, that's for sure. Such a revelation would have more weight than it deserves, Grace believes, adding, "What possible lesson could they draw from what I did?"

My friend Sharon's plan is to reveal the truth by degrees. Sharon, now a pillar of the community and the mother of two children, didn't exactly have a wild youth, but she had her moments. If her children ask her if she has ever tried marijuana, she'll probably answer, "I did, but not very often or for very long."

If they ask about any other drugs, though, she'll answer firmly no—whether or not that is true. "We know now that even one experiment with cocaine can be a fatal one," she says. It isn't that Sharon doesn't want her children to be adventurous. Although her heart would be in her mouth, she wouldn't try to dissuade them from skydiving. But skydiving lessons come with a parachute; drugs don't.

Another mother I know plans to treat the drug issue differently. Janet's adolescent drug involvement was serious and long-term, and she intends to lay out that whole gruesome scenario for her children. "Drugs show up on the playground now," she says. "My kids will know the score."

But what effect will that information have on these children, who have never known their mother to take more than a glass of wine? Will they admire her courage and the confiding atmosphere of mutual trust that she intends to foster? Or will they figure that, since their mother survived some steep dives intact, so might they?

Doesn't keeping your mouth shut and forgiving yourself for your own past take a kind of courage, too? Can't the urge to purge fall under the same heading as confessing an infidelity to your mate? It may feel like the right thing to do, but is it really? Can't the pain that the truth brings overwhelm the benefit of divulging it?

"Honesty isn't telling all," a child psychologist friend once told me. "We should show our children as much about our lives as they need to encourage their own growth." I agree. So when my children ask me, for instance, if I've ever driven drunk or ever gotten into a car with someone who was drunk, the answer will be no, or a variation, such as "That would have been an incredibly dumb thing to do." My answer will not comprise the whole truth and nothing but the truth, but it will be the answer that's most in line with what I want for my kids.

Now I know that this strategy is full of land mines. What if an old friend of mine spilled the nasty beans about me one night? Would my children ever trust me again? Would they think I was a fraud?

It's not an inconsiderable risk. At least, though, they'd know that I had enough decency to be ashamed of my mistakes. What I'd tell them, in that painful situation, would probably go something like this: "I couldn't see a good reason for you to know this. We're a family, but we're also each an individual. Things may happen in your life that you won't confide to your own children, or even to me. There may be times when you'll just have to go on trust, as I trust you. But I want you to know that since I've been your parent there's never been anything I've done that I wouldn't tell you about."

Bear in mind that I'm not trying to avoid owning up to a stretch in the pen for cocaine smuggling. No, my sins aren't a source of horror to me; they're just better left unspoken.

I would also agree with the poet Emily Dickinson, who wrote, "The truth must dazzle gradually...." Sharing the past, at the right time, on a need-to-know basis, should be every parent's right. Abortion is a good example. If I'd had an abortion, I might share that information with my eighteen-year-old daughter, provided she needed and wanted to know. But face it, young children think of abortion only as eliminating the possibility of one of their own, and it could lead them to suspect that you're not all that crazy about them, either. In other words, age appropriateness counts.

So how can I teach these children of mine to know the freedom of a truthful heart if I edit the most egregious mistakes out of the family history? I'm going to act honestly and speak honestly. I'm going to let them see me face up to my current failings as truly as I can. I'm not going to tell them that Dad and I were just talking things over when we were really having a fight. I'm not going to tell them that we can't afford a Nintendo when in fact we don't want to buy one because we think it's the Great Satan of Brain Death. I'm not going to tell them that I wish I could stay home when I'm really looking forward to going out. I'm not going to tell them that I threw the brownies out because they had gone stale, when Dad and I ate them all.

And as for the past, I'm going to tell them as much as I—an adult who has their lives in her hands for only a short time—think can help them make choices with a critical mind and a compassionate spirit, and not a sentence more. Will those choices protect them any more than the unvarnished truth? I can't know for sure, but this path feels farther from the cliff than the other one.

A family isn't, after all, a democracy, where everyone gets the facts and then votes. My husband and I are the ones piloting this ship through rough passages. We have not only our consciences to guide us but also our responsibilities. When I'm tempted to tell all, I have only to look at the faces of my children to know that my love for them, so deep that it hurts, is more powerful than any ideal, even an important one.

Better Scared
Than Scarred

ONE sunny Saturday, my neighbors' seven-year-old daughter was finishing lunch with her parents at a local restaurant. She and her older brother were coming back from trips to respective washrooms when her brother got a few steps ahead of her. A few steps. He made it back to the table before she did.

My little neighbor, whom I'll call Anna, suddenly saw a man using a nearby phone beckoning to her. "What size do you wear?" he asked her.

"You mean my shoe size?" Anna responded, all innocence. No, the man went on; he meant her dress size. Speaking into the phone, he offered to put one of his "girls" on the line. Confused, Anna stared at the phone receiver. A woman on the other end told her about taking pictures for a beauty contest.

Abruptly, Anna walked back to her table and began to cry. Her mother and stepfather questioned her, with growing alarm. "Let's go home," Anna cried. "This isn't a good place!"

Finally, her parents managed to find out what had happened—virtually before their eyes. They summoned the manager, who summoned the police, who arrested the man (on an outstanding warrant). He sneered at the little girl as he was led away.

The parents were stunned. Their first reaction was to snatch their child close to their hearts; their second was to be furious with her. How could she have spoken to a stranger, and so willingly? Even when she felt uncomfortable? Hadn't her teachers, just a few weeks ago, after an incident of attempted enticement near school, spent extra time talking about strangers?

"But I thought that was just when people in cars offer you candy," Anna said earnestly.

The problem with teaching young children about dangerous adults, says University of Wisconsin–Madison's Nancy Denney, who teaches child psychology, is that they have just enough life under their belts. They can undergeneralize—so long as he seems nice, isn't in a car, and doesn't offer candy, it's probably okay—as Anna did. Or they can overgeneralize, and feel terrified of all adults who aren't their parents or caregivers. "It's very difficult to warn children without terrifying them," she says.

She'd advise parents to be very specific about some of the things adults do to lure kids. She'd make it a bottom-line rule to ask another, trusted, known grown-up before talking or going anywhere with anyone. "I'd tell them that most adults are good, but some are not. I'd tell them to trust their feelings," Denney says. "But, of course, some of these people are very manipulative; they know how to make a child feel comfortable."

Those are solid ideas. And they're all we have. But even Denney admits that you can drive a truck through the gaps. Most people who molest or abduct children are people the children know, not strangers.

As parents, we can only warn (just enough, not too much), keep watch, cross our fingers, toss salt over our shoulders, hope—and wonder whether the former precautions are any more effective than the latter. It scares me to death.

The other night, as I was tucking him in, my four-year-old asked how many bad people there were in New York. "About a thousand," I told him; he didn't want a demographic discussion, he wanted reassurance. "How about Chicago?" he asked next.

"Uh, about two-hundred," I said.

"Madison?"

"There are thirty bad guys," I told him. He seemed content. And then he asked, "Do they live near my house?"

I think I should have said I didn't know; bad people could be anywhere. Instead, I took a deep breath, looked him right in the eye, and said, "No. They stay away from here. They're scared of me."

That's what I said. I'm still not sure why.

Marking Time

EXCEPT for my college-gypsy days, I haven't lived in very many places. My husband and I owned two houses—one a little shoe box of a place we managed to cram three children and a dog into before we burst out of it, and this house, the sort of *Leave It to Beaver* suburban dwelling I may live in the rest of my life.

We once had to have the driveway of our old house re-paved. When the contractor poured concrete, we all scurried outside and carved our initials in the settling surface—along with Jocelyn's handprint. Our daughter was about eight at the time, and she seemed impossibly grown-up and self-sufficient to me, relative to her baby brother. I look at that handprint. I can cover the entire thing, fingers and all, with my palm.

Jocelyn is nineteen now. Her best friend still lives next door to that little old house. There have been three owners since we moved; but I still find an excuse to wander over there once in a while, and look at the raspberry bushes we planted and the little patio with the scraggly rose bush behind where we were married fourteen years ago—but mostly at those initials.

The other day another handyman was repairing the cement at the top of my current driveway, and our nanny suggested that my five-year-old son set his name in stone, as it were. He was a little timid, but soon, there it was: a perfectly articulated foot not quite six inches long and MARTY carved in wavering letters with a stick.

I told Marty about the footprints at the Olduvai Gorge in Africa, where a family of near-humans walked upright

through some mud about 3 million years ago and unknow-
ingly, by the footprints they left, defined much of what we
know about who we are.

"Where did they go?" Marty asked.

"I don't know," I told him. "Probably back to their house."

"Where did they go later?" he asked. And then I figured out
what he meant. He meant, What happened? Where are those
hominids now? They're gone, I told him gently. They got older
and their lives ended.

"Like my dad," Marty said.

"Like Dad," I replied.

"Except he didn't get old," Marty added. I agreed. But the
point that all history is change and that change is poignant
was not lost on Marty, even though he is too little to know
those words. What we were making on the driveway was a
kind of history—a snapshot of the way our family is now, as
we had, so many years ago, made a snapshot of the way our
family was then, in another place.

Sometimes I can look at those initials in our old driveway
and smile. Sometimes, just as there are days when I cannot
watch movies taken of my children when they were small,
I look at those old marks and my throat starts giving me
trouble. The relentlessness of time and change is usually a
commonplace; but sometimes the understanding of it is too
much to bear.

I felt that way as I looked at the imprint of Marty's chubby
foot, and imagined myself pointing it out to a grandchild as
my father has pointed out the marks of my hands on the side-
walk in front of his own house to my children. They have accused him of teasing, since a mother's hands could never have
been so small. I thought about eyes I'd never see looking
down at Marty's footprint someday. To those eyes, the date I
notched in the concrete would seem like long ago.

Perhaps, I thought as I turned away, the people at Olduvai

were better off, simply trudging through life instead of pondering mortal riddles. Perhaps it never dawned on them that their footprints would outlast them.

Or perhaps they knew that as well as I do and still figured that the only thing to do was keep on walking.

The Mothers
in Us All

IT occurred to me the other day that I was, numerologically speaking, at an odd place in my life. I've been a mother now about as long as I was not a mother. I've been a mother now about as long as I had a mother. I've been a mother now about as long as my mother's been dead. All those things have lasted twenty years, more or less.

I guess they call this middle age.

Somebody asked me recently how much of what I've done or not done in my life evolved out of the fact that I missed having a mother. I decided to be restrained in my reply. "Everything," I said.

It's probably the case. I mean, it's certainly why I have what most people consider a sort of excessive need to be a mother. To write about mothers and mothering. To mother-around, that is, to act motherlike to my editorial assistants, neighbors, and the birds who nest in my strawberry pots. Most especially, however, I try to mother my women friends. I do that because they're my mothers.

A few years ago, when my husband was dying, I asked my friend Susan just who would help me sort things out—whether or not a kid should go to camp, whether a given professional decision would make me look like a jerk.

She said, brilliantly (she is so thoughtful, my Susan), "Well, you aren't going to have any one person to fill that role. You'll fill a piece of it with input from a lot of different people."

And she turned out to be utterly correct. She, in fact, is the "crisis advice" member of the team of people who actually fill, not so much the role of my husband, but the combined roles of my late husband and my late mother.

I married Dan not long after my mom died, in part because he reminded me so much of her, because he was outrageously funny, had a fierce temper, and loved to fish. For many years, Dan fulfilled some of the roles my mother left vacant in my life: He was the one who was proud of me; he was the one who told me when to cool it; he was the only one I believed when he said, "There, there," or "It'll all work out."

And then it didn't work out, for him. And I needed a mother more than I've ever needed a mother. Fortunately, I had an extraordinary number of extraordinary women friends, about six or seven. One of them gives the kind of hugs that make you feel faint with relaxation. One provided me with practical solutions that have, literally, revolutionized my life. One indulges my passion for wicked laughs and gossip. One is willing to mentor me out of horrific creative jams.

It's sort of a twist on the New Age formula: You are your own mother, your own child (and your own dog). It probably shouldn't work this well. You probably shouldn't share this degree of intimacy with unrelated people. Indeed, my own true mother probably wouldn't be able to be such a shining paragon of coach/adviser/cheerleader/muse as my peer mothers are to me.

Not long ago, someone pointed out to me that this phenomenon was probably, like so much else in my cultural cul-de-sac, a function of postponement and mobility. That is, postponing one's own adulthood until thirtysomething (when many of one's actual parents are aging) and moving all around the map in pursuit of . . . happiness. The friends-as-family model smooths over (and may even considerably improve) a lot of Thanksgiving Days.

About the sociology behind it, however, this once I couldn't care less. I just think I'm lucky. No, call it "blessed."

These days, M is for the many who give me the benefit of their mother wisdom. And even sometimes ask for mine in return.

A Day That Will
Live In Infancy

I stood in the predawn darkness of the hotel parking lot, trying to control my hands sufficiently to unlock my rental car. Though it was only a few days before Christmas, the air was balmy. It wasn't cold that made my hands shake but fear.

I was about to set out through a city of unfamiliar streets to drive a nine-months-pregnant woman I'd met only the night before to the hospital to deliver . . . my child.

And it was zero hour. If I was going to turn back, it had to be right now. Of course, I wouldn't turn back.

Would I?

Wasn't I sure of this choice I'd made against all reason? A choice so controversial even among people who truly loved me that it had prompted more than one breach of friendship? Or was I really, as my father, my brother, and most of my closest friends seemed to think, as balmy as this Texas night? What would possess an over-forty widow with four children—three under the age of twelve—to take on the task of raising another child?

Nonetheless, the adoption agency that had matched me with a nineteen-year-old birth mother seemed to think I was capable.

And so did Luz.

Pretty and shy and grindingly poor, she was already a good mother to two unplanned babies. Six other birth moms had passed me by, but Luz had chosen me over dozens of two-parent families. She'd even asked me to coach her labor. She believed in me.

But what did she know? She was so frightened, so alone. That made two of us.

This, I thought as I began to drive through a drizzling rain, was the first huge decision I'd ever made entirely on my own in my adult life. Compared with this one, refinancing my house looked like a game of beach volleyball, and starting my own business seemed like getting a perm.

This was a big-league lifetime commitment, as more than one person had thoughtfully reminded me. (Didn't they think that I grasped this yet? Had I tried to trade in the other kids after preschool?)

Now, as I watched Luz open her apartment door and negotiate the slick pavement like a tightrope walker carrying a bowling ball, I wanted to be strong. But that lifetime commitment wasn't all I was worried about: There was the immediate future to contend with. Although I'd given birth myself, I'd never seen a baby born.

In the hospital, as Luz was being hooked up to IV lines and monitors for the induction of labor, I noticed shafts of watery winter light sliding through the blinds. The sun would shine today after all. Then the medicine began to drip into the tubes.

She breathed and blew; I counted. The hours crawled past. I looked up at the clock. School was out for the day back home. I phoned my sons and daughter; a sympathetic nurse placed the receiver against the fetal-heart monitor so that my nine-year-old son, Dan, could hear his baby sister's beating heart.

When Luz's hands got cold, I rubbed them. When her back ached, I cradled her, as I'd cradled my own teenage daughter after she broke up with her first love. Telling Luz that I wouldn't let anything harm her or the baby, I was nearly swamped by a wave of protectiveness: I wanted to scoop her and her children up and take them all home to Wisconsin with me.

Or maybe just run myself, phone the friend who was

waiting back at the hotel, and cry, "Meet me at the airport!" People would applaud me for finally coming to my senses. . . .

But the light was changing. The sun was bright at the west window; it was late afternoon and time for Luz, soothed by pain medication, to rest before pushing. I sat beside her as she moaned and slept, my cheek resting on her extended hand.

As the room grew dark, the pale beam of the bedside lamp, the only light in the shadows, enclosed us. We were two single mothers—one probably too old for this and one certainly too young—and outside in the hall carolers were singing about another mother's difficult journey and the baby in the barn.

When it was time for Luz to push, she gathered herself, silent and stoic, her face clenched. Twice she told me, "I can't go on." Twice I told her she had no choice—neither of us did. I put my arms around her and we held on, and in that beam of light, in the whole universe, there were only the two of us.

And then, suddenly, just one minute after the doctor came rushing into the room, there were three—the third, a baby woman, who would grow up to understand all this and maybe someday to endure it herself.

Together, Luz and I marveled over her tiny, flossy dark head. Our daughter for this moment, my daughter ever after. "Let Mom told the baby," the doctor said gently. And Luz, whose name in Spanish means "light," slowly raised one hand and pointed to me.

So I stood up alone and held her for the first time. And there she was, fairest of the fair, seven pounds and fifteen ounces of earth angel, and nobody's baby but mine. I named her Francie, for a little girl in the old book *A Tree Grows in Brooklyn*, a little girl who came up strong and sure in circumstances that might have daunted a lesser spirit.

Francie would not have the inestimable benefit of a father. Her mother would have a crinkly smile and creaky knees, not bounce and sparkle. That was not the best way, but it was the only one open to us.

Still, I like to think there is some wisdom and not a little patience behind that crinkly smile. People might say I already have my hands full, but aren't these big hands? I would not let any of my children down, nor let them feel that raising them had strained me beyond my limits.

As I gazed at Francie, I could feel those limits stretch and grow. She would have siblings to champion her, as well as the support and comfort of all those doubters back home who would be converted as soon as they laid eyes on her.

I made a silent promise to Francie. And to Luz. My little girl would also have laughs. She would have stories, good pasta twice a week, a gentle puppy, and a house full of comforting noise. And, most important, she would never, ever go to sleep except with the knowledge that she was loved beyond . . . beyond reason.

It was late when I left the hospital that night. But the moon laid down a shining path before me, and I had no trouble seeing the road ahead.

Stars
to
Steer
By

The Late Great Me

THE lifeguard is gorgeous. Her legs are wood sculpture, the brown planes shiny and smooth, as if turned on a lathe. Her arms are equally impressive, and her torso is straight out of one of those Obsession perfume ads. As my children and I watch, she ascends the ladder to her perch and lifts her buttery hank of hair off the back of her neck with a gesture that is simple ballet.

I, too, was a teenage lifeguard. With a reckless disregard for skin cancer that curdles my blood in retrospect, I sat outside at the community pool four days a week, six hours a day, for two summers. I never had to save a life, nor even substantially guard one. I only had to get wet once, when a spluttering tot couldn't find his footing on the step. Mostly, I just basked, preening, anointing myself with baby oil. If you'd asked me back then, I'd have admitted to looking pretty good. What I didn't know was that I would never look better.

As I bounce up and down in the shallow water twenty years later, with a leery four-year-old all but surgically attached to my waist, I have to concede that even in my prime I was never the physical equal of this lifeguard. In my heyday, girls didn't pump iron. We didn't run unless forced by a gym teacher. We fought sweat with Soft & Dri and remained slender through a combination of metabolic grace and meager rations of food.

And now, in this pool, I am wearing the kind of swimsuit I once would have considered embarrassingly dull even on my own mother. Sturdy, you might call it. A real foundation garment. With its artful swoops and eye-fooling cuts, it's the kind you see in magazine articles devoted to camouflaging "those figure flaws." Yet, though I recognize the limitations of this swimsuit and the midriff it encases, I am not jealous of the lifeguard any more than I am jealous of Julia Roberts. To me, this lifeguard is an art form, not a life goal. I accept that I am never going to be slender in that way again.

Even more remarkable than this lack of Venus envy is the fact that I, who once routinely came to tears over the least ripple of cellulite, could be comfortable in this nice pool near my home in a swimsuit with hundreds of people around. Yet I am. For one thing, Wisconsin, where I live, is a state comfortable to a fault. Recent national health statistics indicate that 25 percent of the women here are to some degree overweight—and all 25 percent seem to be at this pool today with their children. But the fact that I feel neither alone nor out of place is only part of the reason for my newfound equanimity. What actually surprises me the most is that, as of late, even in situations like this one, I am apt to think of my hips only in passing.

This is new, and has come gradually. I used to be a bit, shall we say, preoccupied with my weight and appearance. In high school, taking our cue from a dog-eared copy of Kafka, my best friend, Debbie, and I called ourselves the hunger artists. We were not anorexic, not at all, but a can of tomato soup and melba toast were dinner. An apple was lunch.

Back then, in my black tank suit and wraparound shades, I had to weigh the same thing every day or die: 106 pounds. Not 107 or 110. I don't know just whom I was emulating— Natalie Wood?—but that was my fighting weight. Now 106 pounds seems like a silly figure. My fifteen-year-old daughter, who plays tennis like a maniac and eats like a deck hand, weighs more, and she's slim. Yet I remained within 10 pounds of that weight for all of my twenties and the merest slice of my thirties. Then the aging process, surgery, children, ennui, and pasta primavera all hit suddenly, like a load of bricks.

For some time, I kept believing that this matron-body thing was a detour I would traverse on the way back to my ordinary self. My cousin Marlene and I used to have forty-five-minute, long-distance fat chats. Once, when she felt stuck in a poorly paying job, she told me, "I'm only working to keep myself in Slim-Fast."

Not long ago, Marlene confided that she couldn't face another diet idea; she wished, instead, to have herself shrink-wrapped. I laughed and empathized in my usual way, but suddenly I realized I didn't have the desire to chime in anymore. It had finally sunk in: This was no detour, there was no going back, at least not all the way. This was a whole new road—and surprise, surprise, the change of scenery was doing me a lot of good.

For one thing, I find that I like myself much better than I ever did when I was a lithe young girl. That girl thought she was ugly and lumpy, uncool and unfun. She wanted thinner thighs, bigger hair, costlier jeans; she yearned endlessly and thought the world's attention was riveted on her shortcomings. The way I looked then, the best I ever looked, was wasted on me. I can't think of that, I admit, without a pang.

But motherhood has a way of cutting through even the thickest fog of masochistic self-absorption. My focus has shifted away from myself and what I don't have and has fastened firmly on what I do have. Four incredible kids. A good house. A funny husband—who can still eat like a kid and not gain weight, but I forgive him that.

Motherhood also enlarged my concept of what a woman's body should be. Yes, it's still an instrument of allure, of sexuality, but it is also a haven for my children, a strong arm to shovel snow and fix bikes, a shoulder for my husband to lean on. Childbirth gave me a new and healthy respect for what this body of mine can do, as did all the other physical demands of motherhood, from enduring sleep deprivation during my children's infancies to climbing up onto the roof these days to retrieve lost Frisbees.

Perhaps, then, given this hard-won sense of contentment, it may seem ironic that, for the first time in many years, I'm actually trying to get in shape. Under the watchful eye of a kindly and superconditioned friend, I've begun doing something I once thought as far beyond me as becoming an astronaut. Running. At first, what seemed like death by suffocation overtook me in the first block. By the end of two weeks, however, I ran a whole mile, and my friend and I celebrated by jumping around like Rocky did on the steps of the Philadelphia Museum of Art. Now I run three miles every other day.

Aha, some of you might be saying, so it was a case of Venus envy after all. Well, that might have been true even just a few years ago, but this self-improvement campaign of mine really isn't designed to emulate the blonde lifeguard—or Natalie Wood, for that matter. I know my legs will never look as though they've been turned on a lathe, but at least they no longer look like they should be turned on a barbecue spit. No, this time around I'm out to improve my body not out of self-hatred, but out of respect. For me.

I run to shape up this good, experienced body of mine so it has the stuff to go the distance. I run to outstrip my worries, pounding them into the pavement with each slap of a steady foot. I run so that when I race my son to the mailbox he only wins because I let him. I run because I want my kids to see that grown-ups don't have to creak and groan, that we can master something new and difficult. And I run because not feeling the best I reasonably can is just lazy—my running shoes are what I bought when I ran out of excuses. No, I may not be built for speed anymore. But being built for endurance is within my grasp. And so is being proud of that.

Love Is Not
a Warm Puppy

TWENTY-ODD years ago, when I was a freshman in college, my boyfriend and I went to a local animal shelter and "adopted" a collie puppy.

We named her, embarrassingly, Shanti, a word for peace in a language my boyfriend's brother (who'd traveled in India) tried to speak. It was the seventies festival of peace, love, earnestness, and irresponsibility.

To pay the shelter fee, I wrote a check from the account my father had opened for me. It probably bounced and I got in trouble. But that's not what I remember.

What I remember is how we treated Shanti, which was awful.

We never hit her or starved her. But we never got her more than the absolute rudiments of veterinary care. We fed our free-to-be-dog beans and rice in a bowl, and my boyfriend let her sleep on his bed. She was barely house-trained. Getting her was just an impulse (like the marriage we would undertake two years later, quickly annulled). I think we got the dog as a visible symbol of togetherness, never really considered her more than a stuffed toy, and were as equipped to care for her as we were to start a cattle ranch.

But that wasn't the worst part. We'd leave her in the bathroom, where we reasoned she could do the least damage, when we went to class. Once we went to a poetry festival and ended up staying overnight, and when my boyfriend got back to his apartment, Shanti was wretched and had drunk all the toilet water.

After that, we returned her to the shelter. She was by then even less appealing and worse-mannered. And though I'm well aware that I'm anthropomorphizing, I've never felt right in my heart about her.

Two nights ago, I was on the telephone long distance with Tisa, the seventeen-year-old daughter of a relative. Somehow, I'd been handed the unenviable task of talking to Tisa (it's not her real name, but her real name is like that, a soap-opera name) about some life facts. Like single motherhood. And education. And stuff.

Tisa has a daughter, four months old. Her name is Simone. Tisa dropped out of school last year and is too worn-out to work. Her dad's disgusted; her mom's frantic. Tisa was a math whiz in sophomore year when her relationship with her sweetheart of six months began to falter. He thought sex might help get them closer together. She thought a baby might bond them even more. They didn't even try to prevent a pregnancy.

The boyfriend's history now, of course. The remarkably frank things Tisa told me echoed interviews I'd done with teen moms. I used to think every teen birth was an accident; but research now indicates that teen births are intentional in a surprising number of cases—fueled by premature domestic fantasy. Fueled by the need for an uncritical love missing at home. But the result is predictable.

"She really cries a lot," Tisa said. "Sometimes, I just have to shut the door and go for a ride. I put her on her bouncie. I know she'll be fine. She's just mad."

The thought of a sixteen-week-old infant being "just mad" made me glad Tisa wasn't in the room, because I might want to kick her in the shin. What kept floating into my mind was that leggy collie puppy, a speechless and dependent living thing, which I, like a fool, expected to fulfill some expectation I wasn't mature enough to even recognize.

But as I said good-bye to Tisa that night, and wished her blessings, I realized that I could have spent the whole time telling jokes for all the effect our talk had. I felt an absurd stab of gratitude that the assumptions of the way I grew up didn't really permit me to have a baby, as Tisa had, or to treat that baby as Tisa had.

I was too middle-class to make that choice. So I settled simply for treating a dog like a dog.

Tomorrow (or Tomorrow or Tomorrow)

I was surfing the Net last night, it pains me to say.

It was my maiden voyage. Never had spent a scintillating half-hour chatting up funsters with names such as Maverick2 and DeliGirl and BonBon. But it was too dark to wash the windows, and the carpet shampooer would have woken the baby.

The only other alternative was doing the work I was supposed to be doing. And that was unacceptable.

As a procrastinator I'm no great shakes, especially given the fact that, in this particular neighborhood of human traits, I've walked in the company of giants. My husband put off sorting his tool drawer literally for his entire life. My father still has bowling shirts from 1953—he's going to sort his stuff next Sunday.

One guy on the Internet (now this is not, gentle reader, an original thought, but these chat places are true and sacred havens for the procrastinator, I fear) pointed out that his skills at the art of putting off work were "finely honed." He boasted that he had avoided two hours' work for nearly three and a half months. He seemed pretty miserable, though. That's what beguiles me.

Since I'm more or less not working on a book that's more or less late right now, I've become a sort of student of this deferring-work thing myself. The task of giving myself over to said book looms in my consciousness day and night, like a glacier, like K-2, like the winged monkeys, like the worst stiff neck ever known to humankind. I am an amateur version of the guy on the Net, putting things off more and enjoying it less.

Wouldn't it be great, since we're going to do it anyway, if we could actually experience some contentment during the long empty hours we fill with procrastination? Actually, judging by my friends' and my own experience, these hours do not seem hollow. My friend Franny will redo your entire closet by season and color if you so much as glance at her when she's working on a real project she wants to postpone.

My friend Ken once built a dam to put off writing a speech. I've spent whole days sorting pens that work from pens that don't, cataloging videotapes, Christmas shopping in June, reading old issues of *Vanity Fair*. These are all nice and useful things, though not critical to the health of the republic.

The thing is, I don't enjoy them. I feel as though I'm hiding in the closet with a pack of Susie-Qs I got by shoplifting. I feel my ability to actually do the task I've made a commitment to do (before I realized that it was hopelessly beyond me) grows daily larger, in inverse proportion to my willingness to do it.

And so, kneading dill-wheat bread for children who cry if you even show them a piece of parsley, I'm miserable. Lying on the couch with my daughter—who enjoys *Days of Our Lives*, and, since she is six months old, can have intelligent conversation with the characters on the show—I am not even able to sort out whose first husband's love child has amnesia. All I can think is, Get up and go do it. What are you waiting for?

After a while, everything—even other work, good paid work, swell conversations with friends, reading good books and long letters—is sucked under by the throbbing presence of the Thing I Do Not Do.

This preoccupation, I used to believe, was unique to me. But I look around now. In truth, my children don't really relish that "five more minutes" they beg from me before they clean the litter box or do the dishes. They're on edge the whole time—you can see it. My friend Karen's husband seems to be under a hood made of the front page of the newspaper, knowing full well a mangy lawn awaits him; but you can see his eyeballs moving. This can be no more relaxing for him than Lamaze breathing.

Shall I found a society that teaches the skill of peace in procrastination? Is that possible, or is fretfulness part of the deal?

Or has peace in procrastination already been invented, and perfected, over long years, by someone else who couldn't face the music?

A Star to Steer By

ANYBODY can become a widow. There aren't any special qualifications. It happens in less time than it takes to draw a breath. It doesn't require the planning, for example, that it takes to become a wife or a mother or any of the other ritual roles of womanhood. And it is neither dramatic nor majestic—really more a snapshot than a feature film. For such a monumental thing to be accomplished in seconds defies logic—in fact, it's almost insulting. But there it is.

My husband, Dan, died of cancer on a sunny June morning, when the grip of a Wisconsin winter had finally relaxed and the very air was a bath on the skin. It was the last day of school, and I'd assured my two middle sons, then in first and third grades, that nothing could happen to Daddy in the one hour it would take to pick up their report cards. Our teenager was getting ready for her senior prom; the littlest, just turned four, was downstairs with Sarah, our caregiver.

I was looking forward to an hour's sleep.

All night, I'd napped on the floor near our bed with my friend Jean Marie, a nurse. Between Dan's low moans and the *thump-hiss* of the oxygen tank, we'd managed little rest. So, newly showered and wearing my aged flannel nightgown—the one Dan used to call my "don't even ask" nightgown—I lay down beside my husband of thirteen years, my editor and my buddy for most of my adult life.

I don't believe in signs and portents. But I've come to think that the atmosphere in a room does take on the coloration of a significant change. For some reason, I leaned close to Dan's ear as he breathed in, and then, thirty seconds later, slowly out, and I whispered, "You are the best-smelling man. You are the sexiest man. It's been a privilege to be married to you." Dan gave a kind of hiccup. Then he was dead. He had just turned forty-five; I was forty.

You imagine that your tears, so long suppressed, will flood from you and your wails shake the walls.

In fact, I merely sat down next to this body, which had been as familiar to me as my own and was no less so now, and let my fingers trace the line of his nose—already, amazingly, cooling.

The front door banged open, and my sons rushed in from school. Sarah called up for me to sign for a package. I put on my jeans and washed Dan's face with the hem of my old nightgown, promising myself I would never wear it again, though in fact I wear it all the time. If I could only manage to see all this as terribly sad instead of crippling and horrifying, I remember instructing myself, I would not break in half. The worst moment, after all, had come four months before, when Dan—who went into the hospital with a little digestive dis-turbance—was diagnosed overnight with end-stage, do-not-pass-Go colon cancer, for which any kind of therapy would be just an exercise. My husband, a small-town newspaper editor, had been a stand-up guy in life, in print, and in death. All he said, when he heard the worst, was "My babies, my babies."

Now mine, alone.

That thought kept me upright as I gathered our children to his bedside, and later, when I told hundreds of his assembled colleagues and friends, "It's tempting, when something like this happens to someone so young, to say that life's a bitch and then you die. But to do that would dishonor the very reason this is all so sad—which is that life is wonderful, and most wonderful for its smallest splendors: good coffee, children who smell like rain, bickering about whether to fix the linoleum."

Dan's suffering was over, but I'd somehow forgotten, in the years of our marriage, to observe the line where his life left off and mine began. I felt lamed, stupid, at a distance from myself. As for the children, who live in time differently from adults, each day was not a step toward healing, but another step away from Dan. Through my wall at night, I could hear my eldest son sobbing, "Daddy, please, please." We commenced the months of undone schoolwork, visits to counselors, fights on the playground. My four-year-old came home one day with a tight and secret smile. "Mike's a big baby," he said. "He thinks you can wish on a star, and it will come real. I know it won't come real, because I wished on a star for ten nights. And it's just a big story."

Meanwhile, the roof, quite literally, fell in. That, and all manner of other bewildering debts and choices loomed. I'd been working part-time in the public-relations department of a university and trying to realize the dream of supporting myself with my writing. Dan had encouraged it, but I'd counted on his support. Now I had to figure out how to regroup.

Get rid of your sitter, friends said. The kids have to learn there's no money for such things. Get a smaller house. And a steady job. My well-intentioned father recommended speaking to a friend about a public-relations position at a machine factory that made ball bearings. "You can't take chances any more," he said. "Playtime is over. They'll always need ball bearings."

Working at least part of the week in my little office while my youngest played upstairs, I tried to put off giving up the way of life I loved. I wrote feverishly, often with two of my best friends at my elbow, helping me when I forgot the past tense of common verbs. Editors I'd never met scrambled generously to throw work my way.

But I knew that I was only treading water. One night, after paying the plumber, I was down to $86. The kids' education fund had long been spent, mostly on home repairs, and I knew that even when Dan's life insurance came through, it wouldn't tide us over for long. It was time to fish or cut bait; past time. I needed to take my hat in hand and plead with the university or with the newspaper where I'd worked for years before that—or even with Mr. Ball Bearings—to give me reliable full-time work.

It was a good thing. It was the right thing. If it seemed somehow . . . smaller than the life I'd worked so hard to try to craft for myself, gradually burnishing my reputation as a freelance writer, cherishing the dream of spinning tales for fun and profit one day, at least it was safer. At least. My job now was salvage, not discovery. That's what everyone said.

I had lunch early that first spring after Dan's death with a close friend, an acclaimed novelist on the verge of publishing her breakthrough best-seller. We talked about the giddiness of her success, and then about rocks and hard places. I knew what I needed to do, I told Jane, so why did knowing that make me feel that I, too, was dying? As she indulgently drew me out, I told her something I'd told few other people—a story.

I'd somehow dreamed it entire one night before Dan became ill, though I'm not much of a narrative dreamer. It was about a big Italian family caught in an extraordinary crisis over their child. I knew their names, how they looked, and what they would do. Given the way my life had turned out, I told Jane it was almost a relief to know I'd never have to find out that I couldn't write it. I wanted her to feel as sorry for me as I felt for myself. But instead she said, "Apply for a fellowship."

And study classical ballet, I agreed. And learn to spot-weld.

Hadn't I just explained in detail why almost everyone I knew expected me to downsize my dreams, not spin even more impractical plans? But she said, "Those are really good excuses. You should still do it."

I'm a practical woman. I wasn't convinced. But not long after, sitting on my porch in the middle of the night, mentally balancing columns of things I needed against things I could afford, I remembered something Dan had told me not long before he died. I'd been wailing about how I couldn't live without him, when he suddenly said to me, "Listen. In two years' time, you'll be far from here. You'll be a writer of merit. But you have to believe in it, like I believe in you."

Telling no one, I wrote for application forms to The Ragdale Foundation in Lake Forest, Illinois, a competitive artists' program. I was accepted. Loading my scribbled notes, a thesaurus, a Bible, and a copy of *Wuthering Heights* into the back of the truck with my computer, I set out in October.

It should have been bliss, the first eight hours of solitude I could remember in my adult life. But I was a basket case. I talked a good act, but who knew if I could really write? Here I was, depriving my lonely children of my healing presence, and myself of three weeks' work, and for what? I locked the door of my beautiful room and cried.

The next morning, and for three weeks after, I wrote. During those three weeks, my daughter told me she was about to lose her scholarship, my older son went AWOL on a city bus for four hours while Sarah frantically searched for him, and my youngest cried nightly on the phone, but I wrote. Creditors phoned. Teachers were dismayed. Even my father thundered, "These *children* are your future, Jackie!" Still, I wrote. I was beginning to see this as my critical passage; there was nothing more to lose. If I didn't give it my best, my family's sacrifice would be meaningless.

And it was during this time that I really grieved Dan, and let my grief have life in the keening of another mother, Beth, a

character in my book, who'd lost even more than I had. I recalled all the agony of the past year, of the night in a therapist's office when my oldest son, Robert, told me, "You said
Dad wouldn't die before I got home! I never got to say good-
bye, and I hate your guts forever!" I unraveled that pain and
reknit it, tried to be forgiven.

Six weeks after I came home, my agent sold my seventy-
five pages to the publisher of her choice. Emboldened, I took a
leave from the university to write the rest. I called my brother
to tell him I'd decided to resign from my job and go it on
my own.

"No," he said, horrified. "No, don't. Maybe three books
from now. Don't do this. Think of the kids."

"I am," I said, with more conviction than I felt. "If I didn't
do this, it wouldn't be showing much confidence in myself,
would it?"

"There's such a thing," he said softly, "as too much
confidence."

But last winter, when the book was optioned for a film, my
brother celebrated: "This is like the TV movie where the team
with the fat kid gets the trophy. You deserve to win!"

Happily ever after? Well, I work harder than I ever knew I
could, and my children get angry when they have to give of
my time in ways they would rather not. When they're hurt,
I'm wretched. But none of us doubts that this is sacrifice in the
service of something worthwhile.

Like most women in midlife, I got the same message from
almost everyone: The key to maturity is to risk less and settle
more. Even those who didn't intend to discourage me made it
clear that, in my shoes, they would be more cautious, more
conservative. To them, I must have seemed a woman thinking
of herself instead of her responsibilities. But to me, making decisions based on fear felt lonely and humbling, not virtuous.
Does a good mother teach her children to be timid, to trade

down their dreams? Does she teach them that loss has to break our will even as it breaks our hearts?

And what is living—in the time we're given to do it—except daring?

One night, a neighbor took my children on a picnic so I could chip away at the mountain of final revisions on my book. I didn't expect to make an end that hot night, but suddenly, I was closing in on final words, and then I was done. I wandered out to the porch with my coffee cup, and the night air was a warm bath on my skin. I'm sure I knew it on some level, but until that moment I didn't recognize it: It was June 4, 1995. Exactly two years to the day since Dan died.

I don't believe in signs and portents. And I don't believe there is any more in store for us than this life. On the other hand, my life has made me willing to be surprised. And so perhaps someday, when the atmosphere in the room changes again and this time the knock is for me, I'll find out it was Dan, after all, blowing those beautiful fates in my direction.

That aside, there is a thing I do believe: I believe in the afterglow of a good and long relationship, like the light of a star that keeps pulsing visibly to earth long after the star itself has been extinguished. It may not make your wishes come true, but it can light your way.

One Giant Step
for Womankind

ON February 27, my neighbor Pouri is going to make a trip
to Milwaukee. It's not a very long journey by bus—ninety
minutes or so—but it's actually one that began nearly twenty
years ago and several thousand miles away. When she gets
back from her trip to Milwaukee that day, she'll have completed the journey. She'll be an American citizen—on purpose,
as Alistair Cooke, host of *Masterpiece Theatre*, once said of his
own decision to give up his British roots and become a citizen
of the United States.

It was not something Pouri ever imagined doing when she
was growing up in Teheran, the capital city of Iran, at the end
of the 1940s. Though she was a child of privilege, she could
see that the rule of the Shah had its drawbacks; but at least it
meant that even she, a sheltered Moslem girl, could more or
less walk freely, without the veil. And even though she would
be subject to an arranged marriage, it would be to a man she
liked.

"There were a lot of rules that nobody paid much attention
to," she says of that time. "We knew that things weren't as
they should be for everyone. But we didn't know how terrible
things could be."

Pouri fled Iran after the revolution of the religious right,
with the rise of the Ayatollah Khomeini in 1979. It was to be a
temporary refuge. Her marriage was ending; and she knew
that an unmarried woman would be in even greater disfavor
than most under the new superconservative regime.

The refuge turned out to be permanent. Pouri raised her two sons in Madison—for all practical purposes, they are Iranian Americans. But Pouri herself held back. Many of the people she loved, including her mother, still lived in Teheran. There was a part of her that believed that somehow her beautiful country would free itself from a dictatorship even more rigorous and cruel than the royal rule she grew up knowing.

Over the years, she often visited Iran. And over the years, the rule that said she must wear a long scarf over her hair and an ankle-length garment over her clothes—or risk detention, even jail—became more of a personal affront. A successful designer, Pouri had competed in the marketplace and walked freely down too many Wisconsin streets. Finally, she had to formally let go of her homeland.

"In Iran," she told me the other day, "two young people who are in love can't even go out on a date, unless they can prove that they have government permission—an agreement to marry." This isn't religion, she says, it's simply tyranny.

There are plenty of days when I think that this country I was born to doesn't give women—especially single women—a fair shake. Politically or personally. I know that a man in prison has a better chance of forming a meaningful relationship than a law-abiding single woman my own age.

And when I was a young reporter, I often heard much more from my male editors about my big brown eyes than about my writing ability. And yet the manifest blessing of being a woman in the United States at this time and in this place is something I forget too often—forget until I'm reminded, in the old no-shoes-no-feet way, by people such as Pouri.

It makes me not just grateful but vigilant, determined to help my children grow up believing that one person's gender or religious preference doesn't shape the world for anyone else. So far, that's still more true than it's not. Next time I despair of the fate of women in my country, I'm going to re-member that, at the very least, we have what far too few of our sisters around the world have, and that's elbow room, the space to make change if we keep our elbows sharp enough.

And that alone is enough to make someone want to become an American citizen, as Pouri does. On purpose.

Family by Accident and Choice

SINCE I have children who were adopted, I'm pretty touchy about the word "adoption." I don't think, for example, the word should be used in reference to taking care of zoo animals or stretches of highway.

But over the past several weeks, my family and I have experienced a phenomenon that I can describe no other way. We've started a relationship that I expect will last for life, and started it in a very, very strange way. It began with my last name. It looks ordinary enough but is actually very rare. So rare, in fact, that I don't know anyone except direct relatives who have it. A few years ago, I purchased one of those books you see advertised in magazines, which promises to give you all the names of all your kin.

We're not talking the Chans or the Smiths here. It was an extremely slim volume, listing about a dozen other individuals, some of whom I knew were already dead. I called some of those who weren't and learned fascinating facts (such as that the migration of the Mitchards to Australia was based on bad behavior in England, and that the name was originally based on "meat yard," that is, the British word for "butcher").

But most of the people I talked to were more or less what you'd expect from a Mitchard if you happened to be one. That is, eccentric to a not-very-entertaining degree. I wrote a column called "The Few, the Odd, the Mitchards," and there was an end to it. Or so I thought.

One day, I found a letter in my mailbox from a man named Brian Mitchard. From Yorkshire, in England, he was briefly working for a branch of his company based in Madison. He wrote that wherever he travels he takes out the phone books and tries, without success, to look up our last name. Of all places, here in Wisconsin, he'd turned up me. Could he and his wife come by?

Hmmm, I thought. Does this guy really want to ravish me? Or worse, sell me life insurance? And what if he really were a Mitchard? As my father often says of a brother he hasn't seen in forty years (I wasn't kidding about the eccentricity), "Sometimes long lost isn't long enough."

So it was with trepidation that I agreed to meet with the Mitchards. And with astonishment and joy that I found them to be among the most delightful people I've ever met anywhere, by any name—funny, warm, charming, and utterly generous. At first, as we arranged play dates and dinners among their three children and mine, I suspected we were both trying hard to prove that the nastiness of Americans and the frostiness of Brits were mythic.

Now I think it's something more than that. Something that has nothing to do with the fact that once, possibly, some blood that coursed through limbs of Brian's family tree coursed through limbs of mine. They used to say you can choose your friends but you can't choose your family; and once that was probably true. The rituals of family were reserved for those of shared history and lineage. That led to a lot of richness, and a lot of misery. Now, because of the exigencies of mobile lifestyles, later marriages—all that—I know many people who have virtually made kin of friends. Certainly I'm among them.

Over time, I've come to believe that what family comes down to is not blood at all but the willingness to share, to share really, not just socially, the things that go deep down. If you can have that with someone who also looks like you and has your last name, that's fine. If you can have it with someone else, too, that's even a luckier accident. Either way, it's family, the kind you're born with or the kind you choose, that you add along the way.

Lucky us—we've added Brian, Jan, Alexander, James, and Emily Rose. And they have added us.

Friendships Worth Fighting For

TODAY, I had a fight with my friend Susan.

It didn't look like anything much from a distance, but we were plenty fired up. I was holding my baby and she was holding her baby and the babies weren't crying, but by the end of the discussion, both Susan and I were.

We had the fight because she thought I was thinking something I wasn't thinking, except I kind of was—based on what I believed she was thinking, which she assures me she was not. This is what most fights are about, and most of them stem from the fact the people aren't really listening to one another.

In this case, it is because lately I have had too much job and family to leave any time left over for friends.

In fact, I'd earlier been congratulating myself on all the things I'd accomplished in just forty-eight hours. My organizational efforts were paying off.

I used to show up for a family gathering in haste and disarray, trailing baby socks and papers and the connector cord of my cell phone from my pockets like a garbage truck, and my father would say, "You have to get a grip. You're going to be late for your own funeral."

But lately, I'd been planning, hoarding minutes like a squirrel storing up nuts. And cheerfully checking off urgencies on mental lists. Annual take-the-kids-for-pumpkins ritual. Check. Answer letters. Check. Have one meaningful conversation with brother. Check.

Monday, when Susan showed up in my hall unannounced

to ask me to take a walk in the golden fall, I felt both guilty and exasperated. "I didn't call," she said sorrowfully, "because you'd just have said you were too busy."

The next day, Susan and I spent an hour shopping. And I was about to put a check next to her name (spend time with dear friend you used to see every day) when we got into this fight.

It took up an hour. It messed up my whole schedule. And I'm probably going to be grateful to her for the rest of my life.

Here is how it is for women. We become our schedules. That starts to feel good. Then it starts to feel necessary. Then it starts to feel like everything. We not only fail to see the forest for the trees, we don't even see all the trees. My friend was fighting for me, is what she was doing. She was fighting to make me see that I needed her, and the space to see her, more than I would let myself realize.

And she was right. When friends and pleasure become obligation, you're in serious straits. The way I've been, if you'd told me to remember to take time to smell the roses, I'd have put it on my list. (Smell roses: Check.)

After our fight, I started thinking about this shoe-repair guy up the street—a little Italian guy my husband and I used to see sitting outside with his friends, drinking morning coffee. I used to tell my husband, "There's you in twenty years, Dan."

I thought it would bug him. But what he said, softly, was, "There's worse things."

Dan died not long after that. For many months, the first thought I'd have on waking up was that someday was right now. That these were the good old days, even when they weren't that good. But in recent months, healing, wheeling, and dealing have all gone into high gear.

I had to call the shoe guy a week ago. His answering machine said he wasn't quite retired, but he was cutting back to a couple of days a week. He was stealing time for things he sensed couldn't be deferred. Mostly his friends, his Campari, his crew.

There's worse things. But not much better.

I've vowed to let the simple and incomparable pleasure of letting the lives I love touch mine more than just in passing. Susan and I linked pinkies on it after our fight. But I know I'll forget again. For three days after narrowly missing a side-swipe with another car, you're grateful just to be breathing; but by and by you find yourself worrying about your hair.

But I'm going to try my best. Even if it makes things messier, and tasks go unfinished or imperfect, I'm going to be like the shoe guy and stake time for my own version of play-ing pinochle at the umbrella table. Especially with the friends who care enough to cry over me, I'm going to care enough—at least some days—to rip my list in two.

Even if, as I sincerely hope, it does make me late for my own funeral.

Intimate
Strangers

Who's Right? Who's Wrong? Who's Mom?

WHEN it suits their purpose, people can go all biological on you. When your sister wants to borrow money, she's likely to remind you that "blood is thicker than water." And when parents want to claim a child, they go right for the jugular and claim the same thing.

Not long ago in Washington, the United States Supreme Court let stand without comment a Wisconsin Supreme Court ruling allowing Sandra Lynn Holtzman of Madison to continue to visit the six-year-old son she'd raised as a coparent with Elsbeth Knott. The two were lovers once. Now they're apparently anything but.

Knott said the court's ruling "totally ignores the biological parent's rights," in this case, the right to bar Holtzman from the family circle after the sweetheart relationship between them went sour.

All the court's decision did was to allow Holtzman to see the little boy during the litigation proceedings. The main visitation issue itself will be decided in the Dane County Circuit Court by Judge George Northrup. The refusal to hear the case didn't set a precedent for other such disputes, and was not in itself a ruling. But it was hailed by gay-rights advocates as a significant victory for nontraditional parents.

It's not bad for the rest of us either.

Whether they arrived by walking down the traditional aisle, as it were, or not, Holtzman and Knott lived together for ten years, and for six of those years they were parents to a child Knott gave birth to through artificial insemination. There was even a dedication ceremony at a church proclaiming the two women as the child's parents.

At the time, it's fair to assume, both women would have considered love a many-gendered thing. They probably would have fought vigorously to defend their equal roles in the raising of their child, proclaiming love—not genetics—as the cornerstone of family commitment.

Now the battle that will be joined will be fought on entirely familiar turf—the turf that divides the "real" parent (that is, the one who gave birth) from the affectionate surrogate, non-biologically-related parent. It's used all the time (remember baby Jessica and baby Richard?) by biological parents who want to reconsider the decision to allow an adoption, and by custodial parents who want to deny their ex-spouse's family contact with grandchildren.

What's really at issue, though, is not nature vs. nurture, but the nature of the fallout between two wounded and angry adults. The best interest of the child is a sort of off-Broadway one-act play that surrounds the big production number of their disagreement.

If Holtzman—who for years provided the main support for Knott and their child—was indeed an irresponsible and ne-glectful parent, those facts will emerge at the hearing. But even irresponsible parents, if they're not also actively harmful, visit their children and the children benefit.

Having seen more people with children divorce than I can, or care to, remember, I've observed one constant: One of the two almost always has a sincere and single-minded desire to blow the other one up, thus taking the presence that proved so disastrous to their own lives out of the lives of the kids.

Only problem is, the love between kids and parents is dif-ferent from the love between adults of any gender. It can be blended and mended and added to. But almost nothing war-rants that love's being subtracted.

Rude and Unusual Punishment

EXCUSE us. But all we wanted to know was whether the piece of office equipment we'd ordered on Friday and were promised on Monday had turned up by the following Wednesday.

The office-equipment guy assured us that he had, indeed, tried to call. But we were out; and his call had been picked up by voice mail.

"In my business," he said briefly, "I don't have time to wait to hear a voice-mail message. I just hang up."

We were stunned. We wanted to march up and down outside with signs reading, TOO DISCOURTEOUS TO PATRONIZE!

Instead, however, we simply and mildly paid for our copier cartridge. For about ten minutes, my assistant Susan and I swore on our children's names that we would never, ever, ever, ever buy a single sheet of paper at said store again.

But the fact is we will. The store is convenient. The prices are okay. And to find a merchant with better manners, you'd probably have to drive to Prairie du Sac or Montana or Mars.

Everybody's rude.

At the airport, a handsome gentleman in a loden raincoat swept elegantly past the thirty of us queued up in line to inquire if we might, just possibly, hope that the fourth flight to Detroit in a row might, just possibly, not be canceled. I was at the head of the queue, and I asked, "Say, didn't you notice the rest of us?"

"I don't stand in lines," he told me loudly. "I'm too busy."

Shut up, the guy behind me explained, and the handsome

gent slunk back of the line, where he grumbled loudly for the twenty minutes it took us to figure out that the reason all the clerks had left was that the flight had indeed been canceled. "Can't you read the monitor?" a service rep snapped at me.

People seem to take it in stride. I guess it's self-defense.

Perhaps I live a cloistered life, but until recently I hadn't noticed that sheer, utter, perverse rudeness wasn't just for employees of the federal government anymore. Now people actually selling things for big bucks have taken on the same sullen bureaucratic face that says, "Just go ahead and ask me for help. Make my day."

The clerk at the fast-food joint talks elaborately on the telephone while my children writhe and beg for burgers. "I'm on break," he explains. There is no one else around. Actually, I wish there were no one at all around, because the absence of any human being would be preferable to one pretending I'm invisible. If he's on break, why is he standing there, burgers within reach, taunting me with his unavailability?

Some people say we've taken twelve steps to this place— that self-help psychology schemes encourage an excess of self-regard and permission. Some say it's the compression of time: Everyone honestly believes his time is most precious, and therefore empowers him to higher purpose.

I subscribe to the domino theory—that things allowed to fall down, will.

At some point, someone vented the basically selfish nature that lurks at the back of every human heart, and the world did not go up in flames; in fact, everyone was too worn and harassed to notice.

The gorgeous salesclerk at the department store is actually painting her fingernails. "I'm not in shoes, I'm in perfume," she tells me archly.

Actually, she's in hell and I'm right there with her. She is getting paid for respiration. I know I sound like a little old lady in tennis shoes, but I never got any shoes because I couldn't find a person willing to take money for them. What Thomas Jefferson described as the substitute for natural civility—that is, simple politeness—is no longer even for sale.

Here's the thing. There was a time when courtesy counted above all else, and I remember it. I thought it was stuffy and formulaic. I thought it was rank hypocrisy.

I was wrong. I tell my children, Someone gives you last year's calendar for Christmas? Say thank you and beam. Manners aren't bogus, they're basic. And if you don't have any, please feel free to hide your true feelings and fake it.

The Long Shadow
of Dr. Death

SUICIDE never has seemed fair or responsible to me.

As a youth, I would entertain fantasies of just how bad people would feel without me. As an adult, I've always believed that nothing short of the death of one of my children would make me seriously consider ending my life.

I agreed with Truman Capote, who (though he seems to have committed a kind of inadvertent suicide himself) said that people who killed themselves really wanted to kill somebody else.

But even "rational" suicide didn't seem entirely rational to me. Some years ago, a man I knew who was terminally ill committed suicide along with his wife. She was physically well but could not live without him. Their children were grown and well-off. But it still seemed unfair, even mean, to take your life, to literally wrest it from people who could be left to believe that their love had failed to sustain you.

Then, a few weeks ago, I got the flu. Big-time, horrible, virulent flu. I was sicker than I ever had been as an adult, so sick that even my children were only an irritation, so uncomfortable that sleep or even rest was impossible.

Before I got sick, I'd been reading an interview with Jack Kevorkian, who until then, given how I felt about suicide, always had seemed a vaguely sinister figure. Though I didn't think Kevorkian should be considered a murderer, he did grim, if merciful, work that I couldn't find a way to understand.

Don't think of this as a treatise on the wisdom of suicide during a bout with flu. I knew I'd get better. I knew that soon

I'd care about food and books and music and news and my family again.

But I found myself thinking, for the first time, What if I knew for certain that the pain would never stop? What if I had, instead of friends all too willing to bring me soup, nothing to depend on but professional care—competent but not powered by love? Or if I had love but was too drowned in my suffering to accept it? For the first time, I considered under what circumstances life would not be worth living—because it would no longer be life, merely respiration and digestion. Naively, I'd never really grasped how death itself, even without the thought of an afterlife or anything else, could seem like salvation.

If all terminally ill people were granted pain relief and enough emotional support to make them at least willing—if not eager—to live and be loved until they died, there probably would be no reason for Kevorkian's mission.

But there are not enough of those guarantees to go around, and Dr. Death deals with the world as it is, not as it should be. He's a zealot, and all zealots bear watching. But what he does no longer seems sinister to me—only sad and perhaps brave, and terribly, terribly lonely.

What She Did
for Love

$I N$ a case Wisconsin always will recall as the "Dairy Princess Murder," twenty-year-old Lori Esker was sentenced to life for murdering Lisa Cihaski. In the weeks since her conviction, I keep being reminded of a single incident from that whole epic of loss and waste. It was the most grim fairy tale. Beautiful, talented Esker strangled the equally lovely and loved Cihaski, Esker's rival for the boy she wanted.

Early on in the trial, Lori Esker's lawyer, Milwaukee's Stephen Glynn, complained that the press constantly used the term "Dairy Princess" to describe his client. She was more than that, Glynn angrily told reporters. Why not call her the young farmer, the young student, the young cattle raiser?

Glynn's words would cut no ice with most of the press or anyone else; the moniker was just too good, too perfectly ironic. But what struck me about Glynn's words was their basic truth.

Lori Esker was much more than a pageant queen, more even than the spurned sweetheart of Bill Buss, who had become engaged to marry Lisa Cihaski. She was a great many other good things, but she didn't know that, or at least not well enough.

Not in her homicidal obsession, certainly, but in that one way—in not knowing her own value except as it related to other people, particularly one young man—Lori Esker was no different from thousands of other young women.

I was reminded again of Glynn's words not long ago, when a friend's sixteen-year-old was explaining to her mother why she couldn't "afford" to accompany the family on a three-week summer trip out West.

"See, Mom, if I leave, he's going to find someone else," the girl said, "and if you get dumped, that's it for you, you know?"

Well, I did know. I could remember, with a shiver of embarrassment, enlisting my girlfriends to drive with me past the house of a former boyfriend, not once but half a dozen times, to see if he was home, not knowing at all what I would do with that information if I got it.

I remembered my friend Louisa, a National Merit finalist, a terrific musician, a girl anyone on earth would think had a gold ticket to the best things in life, spending months waiting outside her former boyfriend's place of work, begging him to "talk things over," deaf to his urgent pleas to let him alone.

I can remember Louisa's wrath directed at her sweetheart's new girlfriend, how she accused the bewildered girl of "stealing" Jim. I remembered these things with regret and with something else: relief that the adolescent passions my friends and I indulged in never went too far, to the point of ruined grades, ugly rebound relationships, thoughts of suicide or worse.

No one would draw a direct line from such teenage dramas to the Esker tragedy, which took place in the parking lot of a Howard Johnson's Motor Lodge in the town of Rib Mountain last September. But the recipe for grief is the same, when young girls get the message that they matter most when they matter to a man.

And they do get that message, every day, somehow, despite the most urgent messages of feminism.

By the time Lori Esker got into the front seat of Lisa Cihaski's car, jealousy and wounded pride had combusted into something far more volatile. But even such extreme ends have ordinary beginnings. Perhaps the best thing we can teach our daughters is that what matters most at one highly charged moment in life sometimes matters least in the long run.

Without making light of the relationships that really do count so much, we have to find a way to let young women know that they count for a great many more things besides, that they are worthwhile people if the hottest boys in school are chasing them, and no less so if those boys are running the other way.

Lori Esker probably has learned already, too late, that she had time to fulfill most, if not all, of her dreams. There were a great many pursuits and relationships that counted in her life. She ended Lisa Cihaski's life, and wasted her own, over just one.

A Farewell
to Football

THIS is Super Bowl Sunday, a day consecrated by television and tradition to the Great God Football, one of several such days every winter.

This isn't much of a football house. True, my husband appreciates a great running back in action. And, more than likely, he and a couple of friends will turn on the game.

And, as often happens when football is on and friends or family are around, someone will look at our middle child, who is only three but exceptionally big and physical by nature, and say, "Football scholarship, that one."

I used to say, when this happened, "No way. Not if I can help it."

But I don't anymore. An antifootball harangue gets old fast, and I've been accused by more than one male relative of wanting to turn my boys into pale-cheeked violinists.

The fact is, we figure sports and games—and violins—are good for kids. Our older boy has played hockey and T-ball and loves gymnastics. Our little one can hit a pitched ball. Our daughter plays basketball and team tennis.

But I get stuck on football, because football, in concept and execution, is war.

A few years ago, I did a story about a study that indicated that young kids who played contact sports were more aggressive off the field, not just by nature but progressively.

It made me look around at preteen kids I knew to see whether football, as its proponents say, really channels aggression in healthy ways or simply fosters it. Nothing has yet convinced me that the myth of the gentle giant footballer was anything but a myth.

It isn't only kids out on the field with instructions to hit and to hurt, or the potential for real physical harm that nags at me.

A story in the December 18, 1989, issue of *Sports Illustrated* profiled Arizona State linebacker Mark Tingstad, a young man gifted on and off the field, who played stellar college football for four seasons, the last of the four after learning that he had a congenital defect known as spinal stenosis.

Because of this condition, he ran a real risk of either temporary or permanent paralysis. And paralysis is just what happened when he tackled a ball carrier in the third from last game of his senior year. Tingstad, luckily, has recovered.

But though his mother knelt in prayer next to her son's stretcher, neither she nor his father—former college wide receiver, former high school coach—ever discouraged their son after learning of his condition. They left the decision to him, even though all but one doctor called the risk unacceptable.

On the day of the mishap, Tingstad's mother said, "Every parent scans the field after a play to see if their son is still standing." That just never could make sense to me.

Whenever I write something like this, I get letters. Calling me a fluttery femme or worse. The writers can save their ink. Given the obsessive chronicling of the University of Wisconsin–Madison's search for a football coach, football's reign seems secure. Nothing I say will make a difference.

But maybe time will. More and more, I read that American parents are choosing soccer over football for their kids. Its lower potential for injury and overall moderation, at least on the field, are big attractions.

If our king-size middle child wants to play football one day, we won't forbid him to, but we might try to divert him.

The best thing about this kid is not his great size. It's his great heart. He's the kind who can't stand to see a bear eat a fish on TV. Would football's kill-'em ethic pose too great a risk to his spine or his spirit?

Maybe not. But I'd rather see him in the outfield than the backfield.

An Abuse of Faith

A historic Catholic mass on All Saints' Eve took place in Sheboygan. Archbishop Rembert Weakland apologized to anyone at Holy Name Catholic Church who might have been hurt by sexual abuse allegedly committed by Father William Effinger.

The mass was historic because an archbishop went to a parish where a priest who allegedly abused children was pastor. The gesture was an attempt at healing by Weakland, whose reputation for compassion is pretty much spotless.

But the healing came too late. If you believe what psychologists say about victims' need for justice—to see abusers admit crimes not as mistakes but as the crimes they are—it came too late.

In the single case that Weakland had known about fourteen years before, when a Kenosha family had complained about Effinger, he said the family had not wanted to press charges. But he didn't say whether he had encouraged them to. They and, apparently, other families chose to go it alone for a long time, in the belief that something would be done.

Something was. With a vigor that may have been unique for the Catholic church of its time, Weakland ordered Effinger into psychiatric treatment and evaluation, relying not only on faith but on science to ensure that the runner would not stumble again.

Uneasy as his actions make Weakland now, at the time his course probably seemed like justice—at least church justice. The fierce debate over sexual abuse by clergy always has invoked that conflict between two justices: one religious, one secular.

Rock Pledl, a lawyer who has handled lawsuits brought by victims sexually abused by clergy, says he sometimes feels, when he interviews priests about other priests' crimes, that "my brain is drifting away to another plane."

"When priests tell me, 'You have to understand. I forgive everyone,' I know they're coming from a very strong frame of reference.

"I also believe in forgiveness," Pledl says. "The biblical prophets would have forgiven, but they'd have given the perpetrator a whack first."

There's another story I read. After 350 years, Pope John Paul admitted that the Catholic Church had erred in condemning Galileo for saying that the earth was not the center of the universe. The old scientist had to recant to avoid being burned at the stake. Another historic event in the life of the church, this admission. And quite a long time coming, too.

Still, even Pope John Paul pointed out that there are two realms of knowledge, "one which has its source in revelation and one which reason can discover by its own power."

Using that logic, what Effinger did so many years ago he did, not as a priest, in one realm, but as a man, a man of flesh and blood and emotional illness, in the other. Those realms exist side by side.

Can there be real healing over this issue in this church, in which children like mine are growing up, until its leaders discover a mechanism for ensuring that its priests receive a worldly whack for their crimes along with forgiveness for their sins? For those of us who have to live by the laws of the realm of reason and who trust those who lead us in the realm of faith, that healing, that recognition of error, already feels long overdue.

It's too late for Galileo, unless he's seeing the stars up close someplace. But not for the rest of us.

My Best Buds, the Brontës

I'VE been hanging out with my friend Charlotte for years. We generally meet at night, when I curl up on the couch. In a moment, the denim fabric, the sensible tan wallpaper, the scattered toys—all are gone.

I'm gone, too, from southern Wisconsin to the desolate, windswept Yorkshire moors.

There's the smoke from the mills (you don't expect it, but this was industrial England). There is the churchyard with its smooth crypts, like refrigerators lying on their sides, the narrow fir trees, the isolated parsonage, where Charlotte lived with her two sisters and one brother and their father, the eccentric Reverend Patrick Brontë.

I know that graveled entryway, the fireplace, the dining room with its slippery formal sofa. I think I could find my way to Charlotte's bedroom, overlooking the graveyard. I know Tabby, the old servant, and the dog, Seeker, who howled night after night when Charlotte's favorite sister, Emily, died of tuberculosis.

Emily is my friend, too, though I don't know her well. No one does. Emily is peculiar even among Brontës, who are a weird lot.

But Charlotte is crazy about her, and I trust Charlotte's opinion (except about Jane Austen, whom I like, but Charlotte thinks she's a stick). As for Emily, even if she weren't Charlotte's sister, she'd have a special place in my heart because she only did one thing, but she did it amazingly. She wrote *Wuthering Heights*.

Charlotte Brontë, of course, wrote *Jane Eyre*, which I like just as well as Emily's book, though it did have to grow on me. Even now, when I know it's coming, the part where the madwoman tears Jane's wedding veil to pieces still makes me get up and turn on a bigger light.

I know how much *Jane Eyre* reflects Charlotte's own life, because I've probably read almost everything about her ever put between two covers. The most recent is Rebecca Fraser's stunning new biography, *The Brontës: Charlotte Brontë and Her Family*, my favorite thus far.

Probably, in fact, I know more about Charlotte than I know about my best friend of thirty years. I've never read my real friend's diaries and letters, as I have Charlotte's. Charlotte is as funny and tragic and dear to me as if she'd just left the room, though in fact she's been dust for 140 years.

I wish I could talk to my own daughter about Charlotte. She ought to have such a friend. But there are no equivalents, in her generation, of book friends.

Not that our daughter doesn't read. She devours magazines and newspapers and the occasional novel. But her fantasy friends are contemporary athletes, actors, singers, whose lives are laid bare for a moment but not ever really revealed.

Our daughter would find Charlotte fatally odd and quirky. And she was, but she also was enchanting.

What didn't she endure, in that nineteenth-century rectory, watching her sisters and brother grow ill and die one by one, until she was the only young person left for miles around? Her passionate writing shocked Victorian England, but she never even kissed a man until she was thirty-seven years old.

A fierce feminist, she still buried herself in daughterly duty. Deeply lonely, she was brave enough to go on writing—an inspiring thought to modern women with crowded lives and word processors. She was not much older than I am now when she died, with much of her music, as they say, still inside her.

Who will take the place of Charlotte—or Louisa May Alcott, Virginia Woolf, or Isak Dinesen—for a younger generation?

It would comfort me to know that our daughter will find someone who will go the distance with her as Charlotte has with me. Charlotte is someone to return to, who keeps the world steadfast, no matter how quickly it spins.

The Citadel: Disgrace Under Pressure

THERE are a couple of standard lines about the case of Shannon Faulkner, the young woman who won the legal right to be admitted as the first female cadet at The Citadel in Charleston, South Carolina, and then dropped out, exhausted, after one week.

One line goes this way: She had no business there in the first place, and the fact that she cracked under the strain only proves it. Faulkner's fold shows that women aren't made for the rigors of military discipline—as the Speaker of the House says, they might have nervous diseases in the trenches.

The other standard line also is a "this-just-proves-it" statement.

It says this case just proves that sexism and the denial of opportunities for women are alive and well in the United States—all fancy talk aside. Shannon Faulkner might have won her battle, but because of her collapse under pressure, women have lost the war.

In fact, the situation at The Citadel (one of its dictionary definitions is "a haven, a safe place of refuge") is more about the politics of human nature than about the nature of politics.

Other cadets also dropped out of The Citadel during the first week of school, done in by the heat and the grueling tradition of "hell week" exercises. There's no proof that instructors or fellow cadets treated Faulkner any differently than the others who gave up.

Of course, by the time she got there, there was no need to. She'd already borne two years of legal wrangling, threats, and vandalism. She was starting a physically and emotionally demanding training in the middle of a record heat wave—no picnic for anyone, even a red-blooded American male. Now add the bumper stickers tooling around town reading, "It's a Girl, 186 pounds, 6 ounces" (a reference to the last-ditch effort to keep Faulkner out of The Citadel, a supposed doctor's recommendation saying she was twenty pounds overweight).

I suppose a real soldier could have stood firm through it all.

However, a "real soldier," at least as defined by The Citadel, wouldn't have had to.

You might expect foolish posturing from administration and alums, military traditionalists clinging to the remnants of the old order like barnacles.

But Shannon Faulkner's schoolmates, young men raised in the same era as she, screamed from windows that it was "a great day to be an American" as Faulkner left, and did push-ups in the rain in an apparent festival of machismo. Maybe that shouldn't have been shocking. But it was.

Had this been a Little League movie, the team, after first rejecting the shortstop with the pigtails, would have come to admire her tenacity, given her grudging respect, and finally cheered as she helped them win the big game.

But this was no movie, and the nastiness was big league. As everyone who has ever watched a war film knows, it is not the received gifts of the Y chromosome that sustains soldiers through fear and loneliness—it is the camaraderie and comfort of their peers. The other cadets would have had that support. Shannon Faulkner went to war with none at all.

If the measure of a good soldier is parroting the company line, as it were, even in the absence of common sense or reason, Faulkner's classmates will probably turn out to be very good soldiers indeed. But had one of my sons been among the jeering throng, even if I were a career soldier, I'd hang my head. I'd know he'd done the worst a soldier can do—he'd betrayed a comrade.

When she entered The Citadel's military program, Faulkner called it the best day of her life. But after she's had the benefit of a little more life, I think she'll be able to look back and see that there was even a better one—at least from her point of view. The day she left.

Daddy Got His Gun

WHERE I live, in Wisconsin, there's a new state law that requires people accused of domestic violence to surrender their guns. Even registered sports guns are presumed to be as dangerous as . . . well, loaded guns, in some hands.

This doesn't apply to folks whose mothers-in-law call up the police station and whisper nasty rumors, only to those who've been hauled in, as we say in the Midwest, for domestic violence, and placed under court injunctions.

But apparently to a lot of folks this seems unfair. After all, smacking people around the house is one thing. But losing your by-God- and by-Constitution-permitted firearms is another. As a result, though the law went into effect in April, it has been about as effective as Prohibition. It's a "surrender," not a "confiscation" law, so it relies on some vigilance and cooperation. The upshot is that these slap-happy gun owners still have guns handy.

For example, up in Oneida County, a sheriff's office reported receiving only three weapons—this in the great North Woods, where you have to assume there are more than three gun owners, given that more than a half million deer are shot annually in this state, and not all by the same guy.

In Milwaukee, a press report says, a warehouse designated to receive weapons from men who've been warned to stay away from their alleged victims has collected only enough guns to fill a car trunk. Maybe that's all the firearms that were floating around in houses where confrontations warranted issuing more than five hundred domestic-abuse injunctions since April. But you wonder.

And now, the snow is about to fall, and the annual deer kill about to commence. Accordingly, some few men who have complied with the law have asked for their guns back, which is not as unreasonable as it sounds, since hunting is sacred here.

What's unreasonable is that some of them have actually gotten their guns back, says a survey in the *Milwaukee Journal-Sentinel*. Maybe they promised to give them up again after bagging their bucks. But would you feel confident that somebody already in trouble with the law for roughing you up would confine his (or her) shooting to the forest?

The old NRA slogan says that guns don't kill people—people kill people. But people with guns kill more people, and more efficiently, don't you think?

Research shows, says Mary Lauby, director of the Wisconsin Coalition Against Domestic Violence in Madison, that when victims try to leave, it can be a most dangerous time—also the time when the courts usually get involved.

"During that period, access to weapons heightens the risk," she says. "It's hard to imagine why people wouldn't think this law was important for a great many victims."

It's also a fact, not an opinion, that the big majority of fatal shootings are not the result of holdups or showdowns or even drive-bys, they're the end of big arguments. A study at the Medical College of Wisconsin last year showed that 70 percent of gun deaths happened as the result of arguments. And I'll bet it's not much different in other states—such as Maine and Washington State, where similar statutes are being tried.

In fact, Sandy Exferd, director of a domestic-abuse council up north, says even victims aren't keen on the statute. You didn't have to tell them that invoking the law to take their guns would only make angry men angrier. But when guns did come in, in many places, women brought them.

As it stands now, in these parts, you can't get a man with a gun, but he can still get you. To tell the truth, I, myself, would not want to be the line officer charged with changing the statistics by convincing guys with no reputation for controlling their tempers to give up their guns, too.

Of course, Wisconsin isn't Dodge City. These are no longer the days when people let their firearms do the talking. It still seems, though, that with guns in their hands they aren't inclined to do much listening, either.

House-
lights

Good-bye, My Ghosts

MY dad's apartment is "over the store," as they say. He owns the building and rents the stores out, and one is vacant for the moment. I am down there on a ladder, washing the walls.

My father passes through with three younger men he knows from work. The men wear identical Chicago summer uniforms: tank tops, rubber beer holders. "That's my daughter," my father says fondly. "She's a writer, and not bad at walls, either."

I fume. I don't mind washing the walls, or even putting up with the comments. It's just that my father is sprucing up this store because he hopes, within a very short time, to sell the whole building. He already has a new house ten blocks away. ("I go there for weekends," he jokes.) It's a better house in every way—smaller, less shabby, and with fewer stairs to hurt my dad's sore knees. I'm glad about the new house.

But I still feel, irrationally, the way you would feel if your boyfriend went on a diet and started working out—after he broke up with you. I stare at the new tile in the small bathroom with a vague envy, as if it were jewelry. For twenty-nine years, there has been a mud-colored industrial carpet on that floor. That was good enough for my dad, and us, too, for twenty-nine years. The new owners will get better.

My brother and I talk about how it will be when this is no longer our home. It's not the kind of place, physically, you really can get sentimental about—not a big Victorian house with a porch children could crawl under or a farmstead consecrated to one family's generations. It's a building on a city street.

It's no longer even, really, our home. My home is my house in Madison, Wisconsin, where I live with my husband and our kids. And yet my mother designed this house and lived here until she died. My old bedroom, now my dad's office, still has shelves my grandfather built for my dolls. My brother's door still has a spaceman decal on it. I look down the stairs and re-member my dad screaming when I, ordered to wash the stairs, decided to use a hose and flooded the whole first floor.

The roof terrace, which runs the length of the apartment, ac-tually is the part I'll miss most. My dad has a huge, square tub out there. If it were heated, it would be a hot tub, but it's not. The grandkids use it as a kind of pool. This bright, hot morning, my sons had their bath out there, bobbing like slippery otters in the sun. The new house has a nice lawn to play on, but they'll never again be able to bathe outside, two stories up.

I check myself out in the glass porch doors, realizing that I have done this all my life—in my grade-school kilts, in my prom dress, in my wedding gown, when I was pregnant. It oc-curs to me, sharply, that since my dad is going to move in a couple of months, this may be the last time I do this, the last time I sleep under this roof, the last time I try to make the hor-rible, balky oven work, the last time I watch my kids playing with their toys in the parking lot below, on Sundays when it's deserted.

Of course, the new house will be "Grandpa's house," too. I'm ready. It's just that the way this makes me feel is the way you might feel after you've had your last child or on the last day of your old job: that no matter how ready you think you are for it, this is the end of something.

And when I imagine another family in these rooms, their laughter displacing the memory of ours, their ghosts displac-ing our ghosts, that is how I feel.

True Tales of
the Kissing Patrol

IT'S commonly known that single moms don't have a huge dating life. It's rare that I get a kiss from a guy who's over the age of thirteen and not my brother.

One is still within recent memory. The guy dropped me off in the driveway; he turned on the lights inside his car to give me some photos of mutual friends.

And then he kissed me goodnight.

"Turn off the lights!" I ordered him. "I'm going to get in a mess!"

But it was already too late. My three sons had glimpsed the whole exchange from a strategically placed upstairs bathroom window.

And when I went in they were awake, and they weren't angry. They just wanted to talk to me, to clear a few things up.

The senior brother, Robert, age thirteen, did the talking: "I was under the impression that this guy was just a friend."

"He is," I told him, flouncing away, getting my robe.

"Well," said my son, who was actually acting pretty civilized about this, not trying to put me on the defensive, "I saw what I saw."

"I gave him a kiss like this," I told my son Robert, putting a lipstick mark on the back of my hand. Robert's younger brother, age seven, made the kind of wet, smacky noises usually associated with old Chevys that ride low on the road. "Whatever," I told the inquisitors. "I'm getting a cup of tea."

Lucky it wasn't red wine. One once told another that I'd had red wine in a teacup, to hide it. A total lie. There were just no clean big glasses, and the little ones had Simba on them. Give me a break.

They think that I can do anything I please. They think that because I'm their boss, my life is one big festival of permission, when in fact they are very strict with me and I don't get to go out with my friends nearly so much as everyone else's parents—totally unfair, because I'm not only grown, I'm overgrown. But it turns out that all I am is bigger.

I used to be a child in my parents' house. Now I'm a parent in my children's house.

I still have to worry who's watching from behind the curtains, and not just because I'm single.

When my husband was alive and we were young, we were occasionally tempted to tussle sweetly on the sofa, as we had before we were married—and actually before we had a sofa. The reason we didn't is the root of my problem now. My children are drawn like iron filings to the instant that my attention turns, actively, to anything other than their needs. It's a survival thing. Even behind two doors, my children can still intuit that point at which my friend Sandy and I start goofing around about something a mother of five shouldn't think of.

"You swore," says Martin.

"You are mistaken," I tell him.

"I heard you laugh," he says. "That means you swore."

I'm heading out to dinner with someone who's probably not the man of my dreams, but so what, I don't get that much sleep anyhow, and my son Dan pigeonholes me. "Mama," he says, but nicely, "how soon will you be back?" Couple hours, I say.

"It takes an hour to eat dinner," he says. "What are you going to do the other hour?"

Be up to no good, I want to yell.

"Just sit around and stuff," I say.

"You're talking then . . ." he consults his diving watch, "before the news?"

When I came of age, it was the middle of the 1970s, and the love you'd take was equal to the love you'd make. But I was too prudent to really proceed beyond the appetizers at the banquet. I'm not old now, but pushing it with a short stick, and on nights when the moonlight is terrible, I sometimes think, O God and all the saints, this is a very short thing, life, to have your children keep you in line.

But I would no more bring a man to sleep overnight in my bed in my house than I would serve my children escargots when I promised macaroni-and-cheese. They watch how I do, and how I do will matter more to them in the end than anything I say, ever.

There are plenty of days when I think being a parent in my children's house is a trial and an error. All those eyes upon me, seeing my foolishness, sensing my fears.

I only repent when I think of how easily there could be no eyes upon me, doting, at all.

When a Victory Garden Isn't

I truly hate the good earth. I know it is a character defect.

When my husband gardened, and I sat on the porch, reading to a child and smiling with approval, I loved the waltz of flowers. Now that I am the gardener, even passages in books that lyrically call the flora by name (I used to envy people who knew all those names), make my skin itch. When I see blossoms twining around a hedge, I think of horrifying little red worms and teeming, furious ant colonies and fingers that smell of damp dog.

I wanted to concrete the yard, like my dad's friend Hank did. Hank's yard is green—in fact, kelly green—and it even has painted daisies. But it is as flat as a basketball court. You would think there would be some kind of zoning law that would prevent this; and in fact there was a small local ruckus.

But I always admired Hank. He had the courage to become his life. And I have not.

I garden for the sake of the children. Their father was Italian, and like all Italians, had my husband lived to be old, he would have spent part of his retirement in a tank T-shirt, cultivating brassy tomatoes. I wish I could ask him what he found so life-affirming about this pestilential task, this slaving on the veldt when a person could be reading.

Involve the children, suggested my gardening friend, Bridget, who once rhapsodized for ten minutes about how terrific dirt felt once she had managed to pummel it into a crumbly powder. Bridget's children have had gardens since they were conceived, and have grown up coaxing green sprouts from the soil.

When I see my children digging away, I want to lie down. I see not young beings on the great wheel of life, but piles of stained shirts, rugs to be swabbed, tennis shoes to be scraped with butter knives, and a thousand shovels to be stacked in the garage.

I see my five-year-old with a glistening pellet from one of the many boxes of potions on the garage shelf. "If you ate two of these, would it kill you?" he asks. I measure the distance between him and me, then tell him, "No, it will just make you have a rash like the chicken pox for the rest of your life." He loses interest.

My ten-year-old, meanwhile, having finished the watering, turns the water off at its source before heading to baseball practice. He tells us later he didn't want his brothers to play with the hose, but it takes me two hours and the help of the neighboring engineer to find the handle under the basement ceiling tile.

Isn't this fun? A new plane of family enrichment? Nay, I say.

The people who say you "raise" flowers are wrong. Plants never get smarter; they never learn to fight off weeds and seek their own bone meal. It is not like the care of children— beautiful and progressively more complex. Caring for them, while occasionally grueling, is a joy.

And yet, the look of flowers from a porch swing, on a June evening, is one of life's most civilizing gifts. So I'm going to do Hank one better.

Not a crude concrete patio yard. Not spiky AstroTurf. Let there be a silk lawn, with complementary flowers! A carpet you could hose off once a week, that could control erosion the way dental caps help stave off gum disease.

Potential venture capitalists, please write me in care of *The Idle Gardener*. I'm thinking franchise.

Tupperware Is Life

I was driving to the pharmacy the other day when I saw the sign: SALE. My car turned of its own volition, of course, though it hardly was garage-sale weather.

This sale was inside. Living-room furniture was either sheeted or tagged. Not much was compelling. But the kitchen, toward which I headed, was Wide World of Tupperware.

There were kinds of Tupperware I never had seen. Cupcake holders. Pie carriers. Tumblers with lids. I ambled over to a fetching nest of graduated canisters, concealing my intent. Instantly, someone said, "Sorry, those are mine."

Undeterred, I lifted up another bag full of containers, marked $1.

"I've already picked those out," another voice said.

The unclaimed loot, it turned out, lay along one wall. It included the hugest covered bowl I'd ever seen.

I snatched it up, along with several trays, a square drink container, and yet another canister set. The same thing was happening all around me. Women were grabbing batches of Tupperware as if they needed it to breathe.

"I need more Tupperware like I need a hole in my head," said a cheerful-looking woman in her fifties. But she already was loaded down with more Tupperware than someone should be able to carry without a wheelbarrow.

I plopped my choices down on the counter and cut a deal with the giver of the sale, all that largesse for about $6. She even took a check.

Later, after the pharmacy, I returned to my office in my house.

"Where did you get all that great Tupperware?" asked the young woman who works with me. I told her. She was satisfyingly impressed. She wondered whether she might not wander over to the moving sale, even though she lives in a combination bed-sitting room with no stove.

"It's ridiculous the way I like Tupperware," I said.

"Tupperware is life," my coworker said.

I think so, too. Once, I thought the name itself bespoke a woebegone matron in a flowered dress, keeping congealed remains long after their time.

The only Tupperware party I ever attended was pretty embarrassing. You participated in games with what used to be called the Tupperware lady. At least, you did then. If others of my generation have come to appreciate Tupperware as I have, they probably don't need to play word games anymore. Just lay out the stuff, from the radish flowerers to the apple corers to the salad spinners, and let people graze. If you can burp it, they will come.

Tupperware now seems to me to be an emblem of a managed life in which nothing worth saving goes green or gets emptied into the toilet by a three-year-old. Sure, it's made out of plastic, but I'm not worried that Tupperware harms the environment. I think that almost all of the Tupperware ever made still is in use.

My sister-in-law Sandy has the most and best Tupperware I've ever seen, and I've often opened her cabinets just to gaze at the stacks of pastel containers of all sizes filled with uncooked pasta, cereal, rice. Sandy has a lid on everything.

Now I'd got myself my own Tupperware grubstake. I took out all of my old faux Tupperware containers and put them in the plastic sacks from the sale to sell at my own garage sale.

I sat around, wanting to cook something and preserve it. My husband passed by and said, "That is the most perfect bowl to take potato salad to picnics. It won't spill."

I beamed. Perhaps men are growing in appreciation of Tupperware, too. Perhaps it's a life stage. When I'm gone, perhaps my daughters-in-law will share all of this Tupperware among them.

I hope they don't fight.

The Power Towel

LAST night after they got out of the shower, my sons aged six and nine commenced fighting. As the volume escalated, and I began to hear what I believed were real sobs, I stormed the bathroom.

"Bobby did it, Bobby did it again," cried six-year-old Danny.

"Did what? Did what?" I asked urgently.

"He took the good towel!" Danny said. "It's the third time he took the good towel."

The good towel is a sort of family icon around our house. It's a swell towel—Andrew and Fergie did not have a better towel—fluffy, huge, and absorbent. Actually, there are two good towels, but one is earmarked sacred for Dad. Even Bobby, towel outlaw that he is, would not dare to take the good towel he knows is Dad's. But he will go to the bathmat for the other one.

The good towel probably cost about $25. In a catalog, it would be described as a "bath sheet." It was given us by a relative as a Christmas gift.

Every year, our family mails back and forth lists of "suggestions" for what we'd like to see under the tree. When we sent out our list that year, my sister-in-law phoned. "I can't read this," she said. "It looks like it says towels."

"It does say towels," I replied.

"Oh," she said. "Towels."

Did she think perhaps I had misspelled cologne? After that time, we haven't, however, put "towels" on our gift list. It's too embarrassing. But so are our towels. Should they be fea-tured in a catalog, they would have to be described as "rags."

Every now and then, after we disentangle the frayed bits wrapped around the agitator in the washing machine, we ac-tually cut a couple up to make rags. The rest of the time, we try to sop the water from ourselves with material that is about 25 percent holes and 75 percent a near relative of sandpaper.

Now there's no reason for this. We give our children piano lessons. We eat meat a couple of times a week. It's just that, when we make a list of necessities on a stretched budget, tow-els are never going to be at the top. Something in me will al-low me to go right into a store and buy socks when socks have holes. The same thing will not allow me to just go out there and buy towels.

On the other hand, a good towel is one of life's small kicks. On yet another hand, I am becoming self-conscious about what I can offer overnight guests in the way of bathware.

Once my dad gave me an old popcorn popper. From his closet, on that occasion, I snitched a towel (he has superlative towels) so that the popper wouldn't "get broken" on the ride home. He found the towel on a visit. It was the one without holes. He took it back.

We figure that since we got most of our now-holey towels for our wedding—which is when you get towels—nearly thir-teen years ago, we may toast our sturdy marriage with a vir-tual festival of fabric this coming May.

After all, the first anniversary is paper. The 15th is crystal. The 13th may very well be terry cloth. Am I right?

Sorting Out a Life

WE have a ritual in our marriage every year at this time. It's bittersweet and sometimes funny and sometimes tender and sometimes resembles going fifteen rounds to a split decision.

It's not our wedding anniversary.

It's the Sunday we set aside, regular as tulips come up in spring, to try to reduce the forty or so large boxes in our basement to thirty or so large boxes. My husband gets very frisky as we roll up our sleeves, deliver the children into the hands of their sitters, and descend into the cobwebby depths.

"The ultimate object," he has often told me, "is to reduce everything to one large box." When I point out that this should be a job for our heirs, to be carried out just after the funerals and before the large garage sale, he chides me for a shirker.

And so down we went last week into the storage area, where we found unmated boots and Styrofoam chunks, trails of wearable items leading to trunks ransacked for a package of skate laces or a ski mask, fossilized licorice, and enough unused chafing dishes to serve a church supper.

As sorter-consolidators, Dan and I have different styles.

He is plagued mostly by the paper. In a dual-writer family, the paper glut, which I've read is a threat to society as a whole, is particularly gruesome. Factor in parents who think it is sacrilege to part with anything their children's hands have touched, and you raise the stakes even higher. Dan began with the easy boxes: mine. They were marked FILES AND INFO, JACKIE, RECENT, and Dan quickly discovered, to his frustration, that "recent" meant the last days of the Carter presidency. He wanted to quibble with me over some things—a fistful of press releases from the National Meat Board, Truman Capote's obituary, an eight-year-old Gallup poll indicating that children were more "serious" than they'd been a generation ago, which I'd been keeping to look over again at the millennium.

"How about this story with the headline WOMAN SLAYS ANGLER, SELF?" Dan asked a moment later. "Are you planning a piece on the link between fishing and homicide?" Actually, I was. But I'd moved on to Dan's paper boxes, and found things that included thirty-five copies of a routine news story on a fire at a cheese factory, as well as a neatly chronological file of all Dan's sixth-grade math quizzes. I waved the sheaf at him.

"That's history," he muttered. "But you're right, it's time to get ruthless."

We tackled the MEMENTOS box. Forcing down all my maternal yearnings, I boldly suggested we toss the blue ribbon that my son's teddy won at preschool, the one inscribed "Puffy, the Fluffiest Bear."

"Are you some kind of psychopath?" my husband responded, gaily trashing fistfuls of my never-finished collection of short stories. I next held up the certificate proclaiming Bobby as the child with the best sense of humor. "Not that!" Dan cried, snatching it from me. His reaction was similar when we came upon a train made by gluing together yarn and cut-up pieces of wallpaper. "Don't even think of it," my husband warned me.

"Dear, we are going to need a bigger house," I explained. "This kid isn't even in first grade yet. And we have three others."

Finding the paper chase hopeless, we moved on to clothing.

Now, I can't do clothing. It makes me weep buckets. Things get passed down, and they do yeoman work—from the biggest to the next to the next to the littlest brother, now three.

And then he outgrows them. And I bawl, because there's no one left to pass them on to, and clothes are more poignant than photographs, more embedded with memory. I cradled my big daughter's First Communion veil. And the opera gloves she used to wear to play movie star.

I showed Dan a little sunsuit with buttons in the shape of fish. Bobby wore it first, a gift from his great-grandma, who bought it at the kind of expensive store only grandmothers patronize. She's gone now, my grandmother, but after three brothers, that little suit still has a lot of wear left in it. Next summer, I told Dan, I will for the first time be a mother who has no one in her house little enough for sunsuits striped in primary colors with elastic around the legs. "Say," I went on, "here's an idea. Let's clear some space on the floor and make us another baby. Whadya think?"

He thought, predictably, that fetching clothes constituted a poor reason for procreative activity. He then remembered that the White Sox were on, so he left me alone. I sort of slumped around the basement. Last year, I'd kept four boxes of baby clothes. I'd promised myself that this year I'd keep only one. You can make a lid fit over a really big bulge in the top of a box if you use a lot of tape. After all, I rationalized as I sat on the box and tried to cram it closed, I might have grandchildren someday. And even if I'm pushing forty, maybe there really is another baby soul out there with my name on it? And say that baby should come, how will I cope if I have no shirts with dinosaurs or sleepers with feet? (Dan has told me repeatedly that I should not spend a lot of time worrying about this issue, and instead get a new hobby, like . . . world peace.)

But as I sifted through the clothes and the papers, it impressed me that I guess I'm just not cut out for the bittersweet passages of life. That paper train was made by hands that will one day single-palm a basketball. When I fold these small clothes, with their dear stains and sweet musky smells of other summers, I feel the petal skin that once was inside them. Consolidating your life means facing the future, and in that future, I'm no longer going to be the creative-writing girl I thought I would be, sitting at the round table at the Algonquin. And no longer the mama I was. Each time I consolidate, I feel one step closer to putting myself out of a job.

There'll be new chances, new jobs, new projects. They'll be good ones, I guess. My children, robustly driving toward the future, are always ready for the next chapter; and they pull me along, ready or not.

But at the end of the annual day of sorting, I somehow ended up thinking about Santa Claus.

One night a few years back, with our then nine-year-old daughter, we had it out about the old saint. She'd started the discussion; we could have kept up the tender fantasy. But it would have been foolish and even unkind, so we talked instead about how pretends are different from lies, and how the spirit of childhood joys lives on even after the pretending ends. She wept, and finally asked, "Will things be as much fun later on?"

I told her, of course. I wondered if I believed that. And then Jocelyn's dad added, "Growing up is fun and hard. Fortunately, you don't have to do it all at once. Just a little at a time."

Fortunately for the children—and for me. A little at a time. One crate of construction-paper hearts and triangles. One folder full of love letters. One season. One sunsuit. One box at a time.

The Pied Piper
of Madison

I figured there would be window cracks. Sagging gutters. Crab grass, lots of crab grass. Even a blown furnace. I figured on that.

But not mice. I thought mice happened to other people.

People like my father. He has trapped ants, water beetles, and dinner guests in his sticky traps, but never a mouse, though he earnestly sets out the traps every year and every year announces that this is the year he finally will dig a moat around his building.

So when the woman who cares for our children during the day announced casually that she had seen a mouse in the laundry pile, "just prancing around," I felt the kind of reality shift that stockbrokers must have felt a couple of years ago one October day.

"I will not be in a house with a mouse," I said.

"That's a good rhyme," said our six-year-old, who wanted to trap the mouse and feed it, because, he reasoned, there wasn't much to eat except rice in the basement.

Rice! Yes! I remembered. Bags of it. And flour! (Store in a cool place.) Bundles of blankets. Fertile foothills of soiled laundry. It must be Mickey heaven down there. Of course, I would not know about this because, as I explained reasonably to our nanny, I would no longer be going down into the basement.

"Shush," said she, who grew up on a farm with about five hundred Saint Bernards, about five hundred cats, and lots of mice. "It's no big deal."

By 8:30 A.M., I was on the telephone with exterminators, firms named such things as Real Dead and Quik Kill. Now I didn't like the sound of such things, but I wasn't about to exercise the same tender consideration that I had advised friends to use with their bats.

I'd advised them to call wildlife folk whose business it is to unsettle and discourage bats from habitation, not kill them. I like bats, theoretically.

By 10 A.M., the first estimator for an exterminator had shown up. He was from a pricey chain and offered a season-long guarantee for a stiff fee. When I dithered, he said, "Well, better make up your mind. It's cold. And wherever they're coming in, they're still coming in."

The second estimator was a comedian. When I opened the door, there he stood, ponytail and sack of traps.

"Hi," he said. "I'm Ratman."

Ratman told me that what I probably had was a "mouse problem."

"If you see a mouse during the day, that is a rogue mouse," he said. "Mice don't normally come out during the day, though they do get around. That mouse was probably looking for food for the colony."

When Ratman left, I phoned my husband.

"Listen, don't get in a stew over this," he said. "Mice don't do much. They're little animals. It's not like they're cockroaches or something."

But he subsided when I, bending the truth slightly, told him that Ratman had said that mice eat fishing tackle.

The man who finally did the deed showed up when I was not at home. He pointed out the air-conditioning vent that was the likely point of entry.

"That's like a mouse motel sign," he told our nanny.

He laid out baits and told us our problem would subside

presently, so long as we plugged the hole with steel wool or caulk.

"Don't use insulation," he said. "They eat insulation."

I asked our nanny whether she liked the look of the exterminator. Did he seem to be a man who'd brought down a great many head of mice in his time?

"I liked him," she said. "I trust people named Joe."

But a few days later, when I had to venture down for rice, I made like Jackie Joyner-Kersee across the basement floor. They were still in residence, the meeses, which I hate to pieces. Even though they are small and meek and only squeak, something in the way they move makes my scalp crawl, *and* it's creepy to think they eat insulation like tofu.

Ratman will have to return. This time with a bazooka.

All Through
the Night

WHEN I was a brand-new college grad, I shared an apartment with my best friend from childhood. A music lover, Debbie would get up each morning and put an album on the turntable even before she brushed her teeth. For that hour or so before work, as she went about her tasks, Phil Ochs, the Persuasions, or the Clancy Brothers would fill the rooms.

It drove me nuts.

I like music. I would go so far as to say that I love music. Some kinds absolutely transport me. But I've noticed that when I run, or ride in the car, it's not very long before the dial drifts over to the news station. It was just the other night that I finally figured out why.

My friend Bridget and I were sitting up late, talking at the kitchen table, drinking coffee (and not even decaf) as the clock crept toward the small hours. "Talk at the kitchen table," Bridget sighed. "Do you remember it?"

And how I did. My parents believed they had put me to bed, but I would creep out into the hall, with my book or my writing pad, nearer to the small light from the bathroom, and listen to my parents, their family, and their friends, talking below.

Sometimes my parents and their brothers and sisters and their husbands and wives would play cards. Oftener, they would just talk. No one had any money for costlier amusements. They would talk and warm up pot after pot of coffee, make sandwiches at midnight and, sometimes, if it was Saturday night, they'd have a beer. They would talk about their pasts, friends who had come to a bad end, pregnancies and child raising, about business, about vacations they would never take, houses they would never build, clothes they longed to buy. I don't know where they got the energy for the next day.

Occasionally laughter would bubble up or an argument ignite, and then someone would hiss, "Pipe down now! The baby's sleeping. Jackie's asleep, too." But I wasn't.

They would talk, and I would listen. The sound of their voices was a lullaby to me, an assurance that life percolated on through the long night—that I was safe. I would fall asleep with those voices still murmuring in my dreams. To this day, it troubles me to fall asleep in a silent house.

Those long eavesdropping nights made me a storyteller. They communicated to me, without anyone's ever needing to tell me, that the true apprehension of life's puzzles and pains is not in the living but in the recounting.

Home Cooking in the
Drive-Through Lane

IT is a little-known fact, but I am the Marie of "Marie's" salad-dressing fame. You didn't know this. I can't blame you. You should have asked my kids. When they think of food their mother prepares for them, they think now in brand names.

These are the same children who once got at least one meal each day made entirely from unprocessed ingredients. When I think of all the times I boasted—in print! my heavens, in print!—about the richness of the homemade spaghetti sauce I made from tomatoes we grew, I want to cringe. (Few people realize it, but "Ragu" is simply an anagram of our last name.)

I could write a column in which I eat the words I once wrote about food alone. In a column about recycling, circa 1988, I pointed out that we ate out, at most, once a month. I now know by heart the difference between a number six at McD's and a number three at Hardee's.

About 1991, I wrote a column about a glass baking dish I got for a wedding gift, and the different kinds of things I'd filled it with over the years. (Okay, it wasn't that oohky; I was making an analogy between the glass and the marriage . . . oh, well.) At the time, a reader wrote and basically asked me, How can you write such dopey stuff?

Well, shoot, I was happy. I had it made. A person who had about one-and-a-half children and recognizable Saturdays. A paycheck that came every week whether I climbed every mountain and forded every stream. Not that I'm not happy now. But the toll at the booth is higher. The other day, I filled that glass dish for a Scout banquet with meatballs I purchased at the deli ("Yes, sauce, too, and I'll pay extra if you heat them").

I used to boast—in print, oh, I'm weeping now, in print—that my oldest son thought raisins were candy. I made cookies out of three kinds of good-for-you cereal.

The cookies my children eat now are, I think, petroleum-based. The fiber content in their granola bars is contained mostly in the packaging, which I encourage them to eat. I don't shop anymore, and my twenty-year-old caregiver buys the kinds of things she remembers from her own, non-vegan childhood. (Yes, I am the Debbie in the name of Little Debbie Snack Cakes. Ask my children.) I once wrote an impassioned tirade against mortgaging our children's planetary inheritance with disposable diapers. I'm still pretty strict about trash and reuse. And disposables have become much thinner and more absorbent.

But let me tell you frankly: I would use those pink "for her" diapers even if each one required its own landfill. My cotton-diaper life was a pool of still water to which I don't think I could ever find my way back.

My children don't watch more TV or stay up later. But there are no longer any days, even holidays, when they look like my cousin's kids always look as though they're on their way, right now, to have formal portraits taken. (I have considered pointing out to my middle-schooler that the green-and-black-plaid pants with the aqua button-down shirt might be inter-fering with his social success. I don't, though.)

Now the person I once was would be appalled. I thought I was busy then. But I didn't know what that was. I thought I was tolerant then. But I didn't know what that was, either.

The gripe about writing a column for so long is that, inevi-tably, you catch up with yourself and have to look your past in the face. The price for living out loud—putting down all the opinions you think will never change, for all to see—is just this: I don't know how I put up with my self-righteous self during the height of my Early Middlescent Period.

I don't know how you did.

I guess, however, that's the joy of writing something for this long. People stick with you, and if they don't exactly forgive you, they hope for the best.

The Worms Crawl in—My House?

WHEN we were younger and dumber, my husband and I tried to compost. We didn't know how, though, and became the first family on the block to attract seagulls.

Now, just recently, my children and I have begun composting, graciously and by the rules. We have a big plastic sphere—which my son Martin only occasionally puts his friend Max in—where we stow hay and apple cores and aged beans and stuff. The contents probably will turn into rich fertilizer about the same time as Club Med opens on Mars. But composting is a good thing to do and it cuts down on our weekly trash output, which my neighbor Rosemary says looks like a month's worth of trash at a Boy Scout camp.

The other day, in this very newspaper, I read about a book by Mary Appelhof of Kalamazoo, Michigan, lyrically titled *Worms Eat My Garbage*. It was not a sci-fi fantasy about a nightcrawler farm gone tragically awry. It was an instructive book on vermiculture, the care and storing of a couple of dozen or so head of worms in creative ways. Right in your house, to eat your table scraps.

Cheerfully chewing in their worm bins, red worms *(Eisenia foetida)* eat two to five pounds a week of coffee grounds, banana peels, and—the going gets harder here—dog hair, nail clippings ... you get the picture. You can keep the worms nicely under the sink, in the pantry, or under the kitchen table.

I think I am not a good enough person. When I consider trying to eat my dinner in the knowledge that a gang of viscous, eyeless things are under my table eating last night's supper, or consider reminding my sons to scrape their plates into the wormerator, I want to stand up and scream. Appelhof, a self-described worm activist, said her sinuous pals don't deserve their reputation as something to view with disgust on the bottom of your shoe. Everything a worm fancier puts into the bin turns into rich, black potting soil. I'm sure her book describes in detail exactly how you separate that rich product from its creators, but there is almost nothing in the world I'd rather not know.

She said further that her own patio bin doubles as a large bench. No one ever guesses they're resting on worms—unless she tells them.

This sort of thing is usually put about by people who want to shock you. It's usually followed by guilt-producing statements, such as "This is considered a delicacy in Urkutsk" or "It actually tastes like chicken."

In fact, most of it starts out as the result of desperation—be honest, you really wouldn't have termites with your beer if you could have corn chips. You really wouldn't eat calf's-foot jelly if you could have Smucker's.

In just the same way, making your own potting soil via worm digestion, when you can buy soil for a dollar a yard, is (unless you intend to pot all America by sundown) just an excuse for doing something goofy because you're able to. Like carding wool from your own sheep to make sweaters for your beagle. Like making your own shoes. It is a thing designed to make the rest of us feel like big, fat, plastic-covered wastemongers, living on processed pizza rolls and throwing the microwavable packages out the window.

There's such a thing as going beyond the beyonds even for good, and a wormhaven of one's own might just be its dictionary definition. Worms, Ms. Appelhof, have their place. And it is not the coffee table.

Twinkle, Twinkle, Musical Stars of Mine

THE stage is vast. My brother stands there alone in a stark white spotlight. Opening notes sound from a shadowed orchestra. He begins to sing. The songs vary. Sometimes "Annie Laurie." Sometimes "Adeste Fideles." Once it was " 'Til There Was You." The song doesn't matter. It's his voice, strong, sure, and sweet. People smile. They begin to applaud.

That's when my brother usually wakes up. In real life, outside the shower and dreams, my brother, like every other member of my nuclear and extended family, did not sing in front of people. It's a compassionate gesture. Our impairment extends to every form of musical endeavor except remembering song lyrics (for which I have what I think is a world-class gift and my brother is not half-bad at it either). But that's not real music, and at real music, all our lives, we have fairly glowed with awfulness. My well-meaning parents dutifully paid for six years of piano lessons for me; but though I once played a shaky Chopin, I now can play nothing, and a musical staff still is an object of terror to me. I have to repeat "Every Good Boy Does Fine" to myself every time I try to read a note.

You don't want these things to be passed on, like a great recipe for French bread, to generations. So we encouraged our daughter, who also cannot carry a tune in a basket, to play violin, and over many faltering years of sporadic effort, she came to enjoy it. Then, when we noticed our second child showing an interest in a toy-type electronic keyboard we had, we moved quickly to enroll him with the neighborhood piano teacher. Bobby has now had two years of lessons, and though his father sometimes notes that most of what he can play sounds just like "Twinkle, Twinkle, Little Star," his teacher assured us that he has a nice, strong hand and could probably play the piano one day. We were elated. Notice of admission to Oxford couldn't have given me more simple satisfaction.

In due course, then, my father gave us the ancestral piano, so that our budding Cliburn could practice at home. It arrived one morning on the back of my father's friend Frankie's truck, and four able men hefted it into the dining room, and there it was, my old friend, my old instrument of torture. Memories washed over me. I remembered my piano teacher, the long-suffering Mr. Chokla, who had a lame leg, and who toiled up the many stairs to our second-floor apartment every week to events that must have made him feel even worse than he did already. My cousin and I took lessons at the same time. "What comes after G?" he would ask us hopefully, and we would answer, "Ummmm, H?" Poor man. Over the years, the thought of Mr. Chokla's shiny blue suit and wistful smile have given me a certain pain. Certainly, he must have had more gifted students, more able, more fully there than my cousin and me. Otherwise, how could he have subjected himself to such woe?

As I sat down at the battered keys of my father's old blond-wood Stark spinet, which probably hasn't been tuned since 1969, I remembered how much I actually loved piano when I was young. How, during a period that stretched from about seventh grade through first year of college, I would sit for hours just banging away, playing "Au Claire de Lune" and "Rustles of Spring" over and over and over and over, indulging in that uniquely teenage combination of stress relief and romanticism. I remembered playing the whole score of *Dr. Zhivago* for my boyfriend while he sat moony-eyed on the sofa. I sat and wondered why I can no longer play the piano, as surely as I can no longer conjugate French verbs. It made me sad.

My father used to tell me, as fathers will, that playing the piano could be a useful skill in life, how I could be the center of any party, how the ability would stand me in good stead no matter what I chose to do. "Cheeeez, Dad," I would say. "That's nuts. It's not like it's a guitar or something." Much of what my father told me gained credence as I grew older, but on the subject of the piano, he was positively visionary. I got a mailing from the National Piano Foundation the other day, and some of the benefits listed for taking up piano, even late in life, were straight from my father's litany. Increased understanding of musical performances. Tangible proof of the rewards of practice and hard work. A great social tool.

And it is, it is. My friend Whitney, who is an accomplished musician, used to give these elegant Christmas parties, at which everyone would sing carols around the piano while she played it. Her attendance at any wedding is sought with zeal. Of all the things I admire about her, musicianship is near the top. It's not as though I picture my own children, someday, in some setting straight out of an old Peter Lawford movie, playing piano for a crowd of bobby-soxers, or especially, performing for a real audience, but the piano really is the most civilizing sort of agent, isn't it? Even if you don't have a gift? Do you remember the scene in the movie *Diner* when one character got up on stage and played boogie on an old piano in a sleazy bar? That's the equivalent, for me, of my brother's singing-on-stage dream. To be able to just sit down and make music anyplace. It could make you different from what you are.

A few nights ago, the piano tuner came and toiled manfully for two hours to restore the sound of the beast. When he removed the outer coverings, things fell out of the piano. An old report card of my brother's (two Cs, no wonder he hid it) and two autographs, one from the old Chicago Black Hawks Hockey Player Phil Esposito and another from a long-ago baseball player on the White Sox. There was also a toy porcupine and a business card touting "Private Psychic Readings by Renee." And a folder. A folder full of all my old early-grade-school piano pieces, with my name laboriously written on the front cover. My son Bobby crossed my name out and replaced it with his own.

Now I hear the little kids playing at playing on the newly-in-tune piano, even my three-year-old sometimes trying to fit two notes together, and I feel something akin to relief. No matter what the National Piano Foundation says, it's probably too late for me. I'm as likely to ever play "Rustles of Spring" again as I am to take up marathon running. Still, in spite of my family history, there may one day be music in our house again, after all. Twinkle, twinkle, little musical stars of mine. It's nice.

Season's
Readings

A Dad for
All Reasons

A few months ago, when the nights still were chilly, our two older sons, aged six and three, went camping. They went camping in the family room, in their Fisher-Price Pop-Up Playhouse. They each had a flashlight and a plastic Ziploc bag full of vanilla wafers.

Earlier, under much close and fairly anxious supervision, they had cooked their own hot dogs on sticks in the nearby "campfire," which was the fireplace, and picnicked on their Little Tikes table. They drank water from their thermoses.

They listened to the radio and sang. They threw vanilla wafers to a dangerous bear (their baby brother) who stormed the tent. They talked about being in the woods and how it would be to sleep there in real life.

They watched not one instant of television. They squished not one particle of Play-Doh into the wallpaper. They had not one major disagreement.

The whole thing lasted one precious hour, during which I finished some last-minute work, cheerfully undisturbed. At the time of day that normally is the flash point around here, during which work, and just about anything else, is impossible, we had the kind of peace that parents don't have to feel guilty about. The kind that doesn't float out of the television.

My husband provided it. He engineered the whole thing and it cost nothing. He's a peach of a parent, he's my children's father, and he didn't come by it naturally.

Men becoming fathers for the first time, today, at the age of twenty-seven years or so, have it easier. They have it easier because they know from the get-go that they're going to have it harder than their own fathers did, at least when it comes to kids. Their wives may have demanding outside jobs, and their own jobs will offer considerable demands.

But as magazines and newspapers and TV make clear, new fathers of today also are going to pitch in on the home front, or else. That path at least is pretty clearly marked.

Fifteen years ago, when my husband first became Dad, there weren't so many guideposts.

My husband was the product of a proto-fifties family. Mom raised the kids but never raised her voice. Dad made vague threats about the belt and offered man-to-man talks, when he was home, which wasn't often, since he owned a restaurant. When my husband's sister-in-law cut the cards at the table with the men one Thanksgiving Day, instead of getting up to wash the dishes with the women, people talked about it for a decade.

Through most of the babyhood of our second child, my husband still suggested wistfully that diapers and night feedings and administering pink-eye drops were the divine right of mothers. But as the eighties waned and two more children made the scene at our house, my husband gave up to sheer need.

And he did it with amazing grace. Though a diaper dragging at half mast still fills him with distress, he has discovered a great gift in himself for being a holistic parent; one who not only does ice-skating but dishes, not only science experiments in the kitchen but head-holding in the bathroom when a six-year-old is suffering a combination of flu and an overdose of grape soda pop.

I used to call him the glamour parent, the one who restored order with logic and planned the best outings, the one who didn't have to worry about getting sweet-potato stains out of sleepers.

Now he wields a Stain Stick with as much verve as a fly rod, and though the kids' camping idyll by far isn't the common run at our house, our children get more pure father time, in spite of the conflicts, than any of us, even their father, ever thought possible.

As a result, I think that all of our children love him, not more, but better than he ever could love his own father, simply by the nature of their childhoods.

"Sure I love you, Mama," our three-year-old told me recently, "but I am my dad's sweetheart child."

I can't imagine such a statement from very many sons growing up when I was a girl. And whatever fallout in family dysfunction and personal stress the societal changes of the past years have wrought, in spite of plenty of absent and uncaring and too-young fathers, we have this, too: more fathers of the very best kind.

To Forgive,
But Not Forget

MY mother loved me. She loved my father and my brother, too, but by the end of her life, she loved drinking best of all.

I knew that my mother was an alcoholic, but it was never a thing I actually said to anyone, even to my brother, who, six years younger and raised during the worst of the party years at home, knew it even better than I.

My father drank heavily, too, but he never seemed, as a result of it, so sick and wan and unglued as my mother did. Our lives together were a process of erasure, which, I have learned since, is the common run in alcoholic families. Awful, stupid things happened, and the next day were wiped away like the ghostly rings left on the table tops.

All that we recalled was good. There did not seem to be another way to manage, and if there had been, I might not have taken advantage of it. I valued family loyalty. I still do.

Parts of our past are comedy routines for my brother and me now. We laugh about them right along with everyone else. We tell about being dropped off in the alley behind our house on the morning of New Year's Day by our grandparents. We knocked. No parents.

We climbed up onto the roof next door and broke a window to get in. And then we sat there all day, eating Good Humor toasted-coconut bars, until our parents showed up at 4 P.M., shoes in hand. We were four and ten years old then. We're in our thirties now, and my father still complains about that broken window.

Other memories don't make us laugh. Every Christmas

Eve, we asked, first playfully, then with increasing desperation, if please, today, no one would drink. More and more people would show up in worse and worse shape. At last, we'd give up.

For all that, our mother was the inventor of most of the good in our childhood, and there was plenty. What people said about my mother was that she was incandescent, that she lit up any room she entered with her good looks and her great humor. And that was true, at the beginning of an evening.

By the end, her light sputtered, the mascara around her huge eyes melted. She seemed a sad clown and dangerous to be around, particularly if you loved her.

And we did. We loved her so extravagantly that we could not believe that two such alien selves lived in one hundred-pound body. It did not seem fair to have such a mother as ours possessed by an evil spirit.

As Mark Twain, I think, said, a mother doesn't hold up to acting in good-for-naught ways as well as a father does. That's true. Mothers are the family glue. When my mother died sixteen years ago, she was only fifty, and I felt grief like an amputation. It was not only that I had lost her so soon but that I had lost so much of her already.

Sometimes I pretend that if she still were alive, my love and my children's love would heal her. It wouldn't. There are times that I think the children-of-alcoholics syndrome is too pat, but one common trait is an overblown belief that we can force change through sheer will. The will to change, though, was not much in my mother's character. So our relationship now might be heartbreaking.

It wasn't that she ever wrecked the car or yelled at my friends or abandoned us, the way you hear drinkers do. But there were times I needed her help, and I would look at her, staring out into the alley, beautifully dressed, with her afternoon wine in a jelly glass, and know that she was too fragile to count on. In spite of how she tried, she so often was missing in action.

Much of my own motherhood model comes straight from her, though. She championed us, she could really play, and she was so tender. Other pieces of the model—my bossiness, my low tolerance for frustration—probably are her legacy as well.

But whatever pop psychology suggests, I'm not my mother. Parents make the mold, but we fill it. I think that I've done things for my children that my mother couldn't do for me. Being there mentally for them, all of the time, is the one that counts most, I guess. It doesn't sound like much, but it comforts me.

Of course, many of the mistakes I've made around my children, some of them awful, have been original, my very own. But my children have forgiven me.

Children always do.

Someday, They'll Thank Me for This

LONG after the holidays are over but before spring officially begins, there's a pause in the year's occupation known as the Thank-You Note period.

I'm an absolute beast about thank-you notes. My children may call my friends by their first names and occasionally even eat SpaghettiOs from the can. But by everything that is holy, if they are not present to present a full and appropriate sentence of appreciation for a gift given or sent by a relative or friend, they will by-gosh write a note to do it. Birthday, holiday, any day someone sends them something and isn't there in person to enjoy their enjoyment of it, they will write—and not one puny sentence. They will inquire after the health of the recipient, too.

I know this is an archaic custom. I know I could have them pick up the telephone. But I have had such joy from the thin trickle of thank-you notes I have received over the years, I have found them to be such resonant, civilizing kinds of communication, that I can't imagine not trying, at least, to inculcate in my children the idea that they are necessary.

This is done in a variety of ways. I begin by subtly placing notepaper on our daughter's dresser. If she puts it away in her drawer, we move on to more direct methods—a list of all her out-of-town relatives' addresses tucked in her coat pocket, messages on the answering machine: "It's 9 P.M., have you written your thank-you notes yet?"

The little kids are easier. We still can present thank-you notes as all that stands between them and a slice of chocolate cake. Somehow, though it takes weeks sometimes, they get done.

I don't know anyone who really adores writing thank-you notes. But I know people who are accomplished at it. My sister-in-law Sandy and my friend Whitney are absolute marvels. You visit them with a gift and the thank-you note is there on your doorstep by the time you get home. It's amazing.

This impresses me so much that even if Sandy and Whitney burped aloud or wore nail polish with lightning streaks on their toes, I still would admire them.

On the other hand, I remember a great many thank-you notes that I didn't get. From the most elegant man I know and his equally elegant bride, not one word. It's been eight years. I'm still waiting. From an old friend so proper that she still feels funny eating breakfast before mass—nothing. And then there was the dear friend who sent interoffice memos on his computer to acknowledge everybody's wedding gifts.

Not long ago, after the anniversary celebration of an acquaintance, we received what I considered the top, the Eiffel Tower of thank-you-note-avoidance technology. It was a printed card that began, "Perhaps you sent a gift, or came in person, or sent a card . . ." and ended "Thanks so much from . . ." The stamped name of the family followed.

It was like voice mail, another of the abominations invented to replace human contact. "The Doe family would like you to receive your proper acknowledgment: If you sent a card, press 1. If you sent a gift, press 2. . . ."

Well, Mr. and Mrs. Doe, happy as we are that you have been married so long and happily, instructive as that is to all the rest of us, I would bet you a silver sugar bowl that you sent out thank-you notes for your wedding gifts and the baptism gifts of your first and second children. And I know that these days you have a busy life, but so do those of us who marched out to get you that present.

This non-note is not acceptable. Please do better next time. Thank you.

Giving Holidays
to the Turkeys

MY brother stretched his six feet two inches out the length of my couch, yawned, and reached for the channel changer. "This has been a very relaxing Christmas," he said. "Just the kind I like."

I looked around, at the litter of wrapping, the smears of chocolate on the linoleum. Had he spent Christmas on Venus?

Then I realized the difference between him and me. We're each other's nearest relative, but we don't share common experience. He's a guy. Most of the men in my family would describe the Christmas just past and the New Year festivities as "quiet." The dinners weren't huge (a dozen people instead of thirty), the parties were few. If I were my brother (or my friend John, or my brother-in-law, Ken), I'd have had a really terrific time myself.

While taking advantage of post-Christmas clearances to buy socks for my sons, I overhead a voice say, "I can't wait for this week to be over. I want to get back to work and get some rest."

Was it the Grinch? No, just an ordinary woman. For women, especially those who work or care for children, holidays aren't respite—they're contests, marathons, sunup-to-sundown bouts of the nurturance we provide in sprint form every day of the year. That's true even if you skip the clove oranges, buy the ham precooked, and don't sent cards.

My friend Stacey's boyfriend was dismayed to hear that she was planning to go to Arizona and sit by a pool at Thanksgiving. "Shoot," he said, "that's my favorite holiday."

Stacey let him have it. "Of course it is," she told him. "You don't have to shop after work for two weeks, start cooking two days in advance, get up in the middle of the night to start a turkey, set a table and serve a meal, spend the next few hours making coffee and washing dishes, and then hear your beloved say, 'Why can't you just enjoy yourself?' "

"If you don't enjoy it," he said mildly, "you shouldn't do it."

But then what would happen? According to my kin, I'm already in something less than a state of domestic grace.

My father, as near as I can figure it, has never cooked a meal or wrapped a gift. Still, he complains that Christmas is too hectic. He pointed out that my sister-in-law and I warmed but forgot to serve the stuffing, as we rushed about trying to mount a feast, care for five children, and not disturb the Green Bay Packer telecast.

"Young women today have too much on their minds," he said, in what I suppose was intended as a statement of wistful tolerance. I fantasized about my father wearing the stuffing, still in its ornate bowl, upside-down like a hat.

My brother and I trade holidays. One year, Thanksgiving is at his house, the next year at mine. One year, we head down to Illinois to welcome Santa, the next year they come here. What I propose is this: Let's carry out that plan on an intergender scale. One year, the women will do the holidays: cook, shop, stage-manage, and serve. The next year, the men of a family can do everything.

I know that my brother and my friend John, who are engineers, can figure out time-saving strategies to make the meals and gatherings go more smoothly. I know they will not mind if my sisters-in-law and my female friends ask, "Do you have any horseradish sauce?" as if we were in a restaurant. I know they won't mind bringing us a glass of ice water so that we don't have to get up from the table.

Then, maybe just once before I die, I'll be able to truly love a holiday. A day in which all I have to decide is whether too many handfuls of cashews will spoil my dinner. A time of magic, when I don't know what is in every single package—including the ones for me. I'll be able to experience holidays with the wonder of a child.

Or a grown man.

Let There Be Lights

I wish the Christmas season lasted six months—minimum. Now don't get worried. This isn't going to be one of those columns that make your fillings hurt, about how if all of us could keep that spirit of wonder and magic and childlike joy throughout the year, what a darn nice world this would be.

You can hardly argue with the idea, but if the price of universal goodwill was six solid months of commercials featuring polar bears drinking Cokes, I'd sooner pass.

What I hate to see go are the lights.

All but the most severely affected decomaniacs in my neighborhood have their lights down by now. My mother used to insist on leaving them up until what she called "Old Christmas," which is, I guess, the Feast of Epiphany, traditionally, January 6. The Russian Orthodox Christmas also comes in January, and the way my mother felt about lights, if she had known it, she probably would have left them up for that, too.

I feel the same way, although I took my lights down on New Year's morning because otherwise, I feared, I might leave them up forever. There were a slew of them—blinking lights, chasing lights, fat multicolored lights. One neighbor, who said she expected to hear a Jimi Hendrix recording pulsing away whenever she passed, suggested we went so indiscriminately festive because of our kids. I went along with her. But I'm the real culprit.

There's something about strings of lights. Perhaps it's the nature of light itself, the comfort provided by that universal symbol of safety and grace. No matter how forlorn the house, lights make a brave show. I put up lights at any excuse, even for Halloween. I'd put them up for Valentine's Day and Lincoln's birthday, too, if I didn't think people would stare.

A string of lights is like a great haircut or an expensive tie. It draws attention away from the rest of the package. It doesn't matter if the rest is held together with safety pins. It's the flash that counts. Without the lights, we just have a porch that needs paint and windows that need washing, overlooking a vista of snow in tones of white, yellow, and gray.

Taking down the lights is the symbol, for me, of the real beginning of winter. Not the lovely marshmallow December winter, a sort of store-window novelty time. No, I mean the long, bone-deep, Wisconsin season that is more to be survived than savored.

People on the corner near a house where I once lived used to leave their lights up until April and turn them on every night. I used to make up stories about them: They had a kid in the service who couldn't get home until the new year; or someone had been stricken, and people just let the unimportant chores go. Just before we moved, figuring I'd never see the old man who lived there again, I asked him about the lights. "We just like the way they make the night look," he said.

Eccentric? Sure. But for about $20 and a few nails, he'd been able to hold back the long winter's night until the long winter's night was almost gone. I understood. I understood.

Just Before Dark

SATURDAY was the designated day. The last good-bye of the long good-bye season—the day we'd put the yard to bed for the winter. When I rolled my sons out of bed and put rakes and trowels in their hands, one was already prepared with what he thought was a surefire excuse.

"I heard on the radio, Mom," he said, "you're not supposed to cover your roses yet, or even cut them back."

The plant maven, it turns out, had said to wait until the ground froze solid and then lump the dirt over the top of the roses. But it felt like winter to me; the geese were long gone, the morning ground furred with gray frost.

I lopped off my roses and lumped dirt over their heads in forty-degree sunshine, confident that the roses would make it. After all, these roses are Wisconsin, just as I am. I think they wanted to pull the blanket of earth over their heads, just as I want to pull the comforter over mine every time we face another dark dawn.

My grandmother, who had rural roots, called November the "gathering-in" time. I don't have anything except my children, from the dark street at twilight, to gather in. But the urgency I feel is real.

The rituals of readiness for winter have become very important to me, much as I, my back, my fingernails, and my children hate them. To have winter catch us unprepared—with water still in our outside pipes, with rose tips still looking for light, with bulbs unmulched by a bedding of straw, that would feel so un-Wisconsin.

And so we gave up the last temperate day of the year to toting around bundles of straw, stacking sticks at the curbside, shoveling banks of dirt. If those stacks and sticks and stalks could speak, they'd swear, because that's what I did, under my breath, as I toted and spread and dug and drained.

Now, however, I'm satisfied with the way we have erased summer from our yard, put it to sleep with a pat and a hope. I sit on the porch at night, and I'm the only thing out there not covered with tarps and strapping tape. We are battened down, protected, nothing can blow away our picnic table or our next year's irises. At least, nothing we can imagine.

Of course, the reason I feel so satisfied is the result of a mental trick. It's not bulbs or lawn furniture I'm really concerned about. My nature rebels against replacing them, but they're all replaceable. Though doing all these things is my practical responsibility as a homeowner, more important, doing them is my psychological responsibility as a homemaker.

Just the act of readying my house for winter seems also to ready my home. It's a gesture of propitiation to the winter gods, a promise that I can protect me and mine against the keenest wind and the most harrowing cold—if I'm careful, if I'm prudent. As prudent as all mother mammals stocking up the den. Every year, we seem always to be racing against time, against failing light, against an ever-more-insistent north wind.

Every year, we feel we've barely made it, that we've closed the door against a vague danger. Every year, the inside of our house, which looks drab and uninviting compared with the green-and-blue riot outside during the summer months, begins to look inviting, forgiving. Like a place that could take you in.

Now the yard is completely uglified, stark except for the piles of mulch I'll remove in dirty dripping heaps on some spring afternoon I can't quite imagine will ever come again. Letting go of the outside of the house is sad; and yet I feel safe.

We're ready for it now. Let it come.

Each Day's Joy

I remember what my mother used to say to me when I was very young and she was settling me down for the night.

"You need to get a good night's sleep now," she would tell me, "because, remember, tomorrow . . ."

And then, voice animated and eyes wide, she would tell me what we were going to do the next day. Big, important stuff. We were going to get a new collar for the dog. Or, after school, we were going to drive through the arboretum.

Now I'm wise to her trick. She was trying to get me to go to sleep without fussing. I do the same thing when I tuck my children in. Only rarely do I have anything momentous to promise for the morrow. Once in a while we're going to leave early to go out of town. More often, I'll say something like "Tomorrow, we're going to plant tomato seeds. Tomorrow you can take your top to show your friends at school."

It took me years to see that there was more to this than a soothing way to get children to give up one day in anticipation of the next. What my mother was doing was giving me something to hang my dreams on. She also was giving me the essence of her nature, which was hopeful.

For a long time, that wasn't my own nature. I spent years of my life waiting for what I called "the next big thing" to happen. I still do. But it's a game. I'm not going to win the lottery or get summoned to Hollywood to write screenplays for Meryl Streep.

But tomorrow we are going to plant some new lilac bushes.

I might get a long-awaited check in the mail. Those will be good things. This is what my mother gave me.

She gave me the sense to appreciate light traffic, spaghetti for dinner, a good book waiting upstairs. There always would be a jewel in the ordinary clay of work or school.

In the Bible it says that each day's evil is sufficient to that day. What my mother believed, without being an overbearing Pollyanna about it, is that so is each day's joy. There might be only a little. The look of the sky before a storm. Getting all the laundry done. But something.

She sensed—and taught me—that the aggregate of all the little things is, finally, all we have. Big things don't turn up often enough to spend time pining after them. Ordinary life is the big thing. She had the knack of appreciating it.

And that's a knack we want to give our children early on. Every day is not going to bring a trip to the toy store or even a rental video. But every day, if you slow down long enough to look for it, will bring something. Any excuse to celebrate, even the smallest, was a good enough excuse the way my mother reckoned it.

So even in the blackest periods of my life, there always was the chance that something could turn out interesting, tomorrow.

Our children are growing up in a difficult world. One of the most difficult things about that world is that too much is offered and too much is expected. As I tuck them in at night, I want to remind them, by holding out the smallest possible cause for joy, of a way to keep their boundaries manageable, so that the world will not crush them, so that it will not take too much to buoy them up when they are sad.

Last night, my seven-year-old reminded me that, yep, tomorrow was the day we'd paint the handlebars on his bike. And so we will. And if my mother were still alive, I expect she'd want to help.

The Quality of Mercy
Is Still Strained

THIS year, I hold the indoor record for attending performances of our city theater's production of *A Christmas Carol*.

My son who's thirteen plays one of the Cratchit children. Not an over-doting parent, I only purchased one hundred or so tickets, one for every friend, relative, and minor acquaintance in the Midwest. Still, after two nights of marveling that my son could even pretend to be a kid who said things such as "Yes, Mother," I needed distraction to survive four more performances.

A Christmas Carol is hardly cutting-edge drama—in fact, lots of people find it sappy. But heavy-handed as he could be, Charles Dickens was a zealot for social reform. Thus, the story's not about Christmas or Christian duty (though there's a fair amount of religious talk in it), but about poor people— the responsibility of them, the danger of them, the horror of them. Dickens would have devoured newspapers these days. Plenty of stories lately zero in on precisely the same topic, social reform having to do with poor people.

However, prevailing opinion about the issue is sort of Dickens's message turned inside out. He aimed to shame nineteenth-century Londoners into caring for the unfed, underemployed, and desperate. But today's pundits and lawmakers are wringing their hands in vexation because charity evidently has gotten out of hand, and people are fed up with wantonly pouring money to aid families that don't support themselves.

Then and now, though, charity never really had a great

reputation. People who need it don't want to admit getting it. The rest of us sometimes feel guilty and resentful about having to give it.

Back in Victorian England, London streets swarmed with dirty, skinny urchins, begging for coins. The panhandlers today who accost shoppers exiting glittering stores on Fifth Avenue aren't really so different, except few of them are children.

Still, I've spent so many nights listening to Dickens's morality play I'm starting to feel as haunted as Ebenezer Scrooge. I wince when the Ghost of Christmas Present says, "It may be, that in the sight of Heaven, you are more worthless and less fit to live than millions like this poor man's child."

And those gruesome specters, the boy called Ignorance and the girl called Want: "Most of all, beware this boy," the ghost says. "That which I see written on his brow is Doom!" I jumped when my seven-year-old, wiggling in his seat, whispered to me, "He means that kid is going to grow up and kill people."

It gave me shivers. But as a politician friend of mine said recently, "I've never seen anybody willingly sit down on the curb and starve to death." Whether they're diligent but unlucky, crazy or lazy, people need what they need. The good who don't get it will suffer. The bad will just take it. All those Christmas spirits agreed: Ignore them now, you'll deal with them later.

Early in the play, Scrooge's nephew Fred says the glory of this season is that fortunate people regard the disadvantaged as fellow passengers instead of "another race of creatures." The hard part is remembering the rest of the year that people without means have the same dreams.

It would be nice for all poor folk to get their lives in gear as a result of getting off the welfare train. Some surely will. Others will just slide further into hell.

Ah, hell. The only thing that still (after five performances) scares my younger children is Marley's ghost rattling his chain made of keys and safety-deposit boxes. You don't have to believe in eternal life to wonder if turning away from want is a weight on the spirit.

I sit in the dark and watch Ebenezer's anguish. And it chills me to think of a Christmas yet to come when a whole society might have to regret Scrooging up its soul.

The Great Green
Garage Sale

MY agreement with this newspaper prohibits me from writing about a few subjects more than once a year. Chief among those is garage sales.

I now have transcended the period of my life when the price of material goods was so shocking to me that I virtually could not purchase anything at retail. But my affinity for garage sales—as community gatherings, as the ecologically sound alternative to department-store consumption, as cheap thrills—has not diminished.

Grabbing up one or more of my children and making an aimless round on Saturday mornings, picking up a few T-shirts and a trivet for a total of $3.50, has sustained me over some of the roughest periods of my life. Some women rush out for acrylic nails. Some buy suits. I want the charge, but not the guilty repercussions. Even given all that, it wasn't until a recent experience that I realized garage sales have a spiritual dimension as well.

Susan, a friend, was moving, and she enlisted the help of others to mount a garage sale before the eventful day. Susan, who considers the Field Days sale about as close as she'd ever come to the world of rummage, is not really the garage-sale type. She wanted to mark everything thirty cents. Then she wanted to mark everything $5. When the dawn came up like thunder on the great day, Susan, who had not slept most of the previous night, was distraught.

People were swarming and dickering. People were knocking over and dropping. People were paying full price for napkin rings and offering $2 for $75 sofas. But no one was buying what Susan really wanted to recycle—her daughter's gorgeous baby clothes, all appliquéed with the kinds of sweet ducks and bunnies that Margot would now, at seven, stuff behind a potted plant.

Then, just before the day ended, a woman drove up. Her car clattered to a stop, and she and her husband climbed out with their baby girl. She was a pretty little thing, and her mother snatched up the clothes in delight, holding one thing after another up to the child's chin. Finally, though, she carefully selected only one dress and one shirt, telling her husband firmly that they couldn't afford more. "They're lovely clothes," she told Susan. "Thank you so much."

As she was walking away, Susan made a snap judgment, running after the woman with armfuls of clothing. It wasn't playing Lady Bountiful that gave Susan such a glow. It was the gift of feeling something you loved had moved down the line to be loved again. It was passing along a kind of grace.

Susan probably realized about $27 from her sale. But she felt wealthy.

In reverse, the same thing happened to me. I came upon on a garage sale that featured clothing in my size. I pillaged the place, filling a trash bag for $25.

The next morning, at the sort-of-ritzy preschool my youngest attends, I passed the father. I figured he didn't recognize me—partly because he never looked at my face. I was wearing his wife's blouse, skirt, and shoes. The next day, the same thing happened. This time he grinned.

Embarrassing? Not at all. It was a link, safe but mutually gratifying.

Death Takes
a Holiday

IT'S Halloween and the whole neighborhood looks like a cemetery.

There are white ranks of tombstones on my neighbors' lawn—one for every person in the family. Skeletons rustle in the trees, and one of my friends even made a Barbie sarcophagus for his little girl.

It's all in good fun, though. And this is the first year in several that my kids and I have been able to appreciate it.

For the past two Halloweens, since my husband died, we were not offended, not at all, but unsettled by the trappings of what once was our very favorite holiday.

After all, Halloween is a festival of death, both in terms of its ancient roots and in its modern-day incarnation. It's a sort of harvest-time whistle in the dark at surviving the dying light at the dying time of year, a comic-sinister interlude exploring what lies beyond and hoping to avoid it for the time being.

Last year, when the tombstones began sprouting in the yards and the ghost lights twinkled on the evergreens, my sons and I felt funny.

Death, after all, was a member of our family. For us, "Rest in Peace" wasn't a sort of Disney haunted-house legend, but the genuine thing. We understood how our friends, who mostly are Jewish, feel when someone slips up and wishes them a festive "Merry Christmas." Not angry, but odd.

It had been a year when my oldest son, who had inherited his Uncle Charley's Grim Reaper robe and mask, decided to go trick-or-treating as a construction worker instead.

But now another year has unfurled, and though death is still more an intimate acquaintance than we would wish it to be at this point in our lives, the edge has been rubbed off the poignancy by the wearing wheel of the seasons.

When we got out the costumes from the cardboard box this year, my oldest son decided that for this, his "last" year of trick-or-treat (he has declared this, solemnly, since he was nine), he would indeed go as the Grim Reaper.

"Do you know where I can buy a scythe?" he asked me without irony. My middle son is going to be Dracula, the littlest a prisoner wearing a ball and chain. Though we can't quite put tombstones up in our yard, we do have a lovely purple Frankenstein's monster.

The other day, the Tiger Cub Scouts were meeting in our yard. And one little boy asked my son Martin what the plaque under our little birch tree meant.

"The tree was planted for my dad by the people at his newspaper," Martin said. "He died."

"Is that his grave? Is he under there?" asked the young friend. I trembled, but kept silent.

"No, but some of his ashes are," Martin explained evenly.

"Does that mean he could rise up on Halloween and go get the mail out of the mailbox?" his friend asked.

Martin laughed. "That would be neat," he said.

And, you know, it would be neat. I couldn't think of a ghost I'd rather have haunt this house. But the healing thing for me wasn't the giggly reference, but the giggles themselves. Not forced, not frightened. Just six-year-old frankness.

It's Halloween, and once again we can laugh at death. Just the way all people do. That doesn't mean that we've forgotten. It means we've gone on living.

The Sheer Joy
of Nothing Much

THERE are days that lock into your memory as they happen. You know, even at the moment, that they will be there forever and you won't need to refresh them with pictures from an album.

The day you marry or first set eyes on your newborn child—those are obvious ones. The day you get a phone call about a new job that makes everything else possible is another.

And then there are all of those others, of course, the ones that crowd around when you're trying to fall asleep, the stormy, stressful days that you remember as you strive to forget.

This was an ordinary day, a Sunday, the day that for me usually seems weeks long, weeks of unsorted laundry and niggling deadlines, with Monday and its obligations menacing from the wings.

This was just a Sunday. My father was visiting from Chicago. We took the children to church, and even the obligatory wailing about wearing something other than tennis shoes was more funny than tense. At church, the choir sang so well that the congregation spontaneously applauded. We picked up muffins on the way home.

After lunch, we took kites to the field behind the house. The baby waddled to the top of a knoll and fell, rolling over and over. When we got to him, panicked, he was laughing.

Our six-year-old ran up the hill with his dragon kite behind him, just playing really, but suddenly the kite went aloft, and he was frozen in concentration, letting out the string just the right way. My father was guiding him, gently, not annoyed or impatient, the way those once removed from parenthood can get sometimes.

When my son let the kite falter, my father ran to him, ran all out, the way he doesn't do much anymore, and righted the flight. From below, I watched the two of them, my son's bright buttermilk hair above his red parka. I could hear snatches of their teasing brought to me by the wind, see my father cuff my son playfully, and there is no describing it.

We went back home, collected more of the family, and visited a park, where a vendor gave each of the children a yellow balloon for free. And the afternoon got hotter. It was spring after all, and even the days of freezing drizzle that undoubtedly would follow could not take it away. The children brought their coats for me to hold and attacked the playground equipment with pure animal eagerness, running and climbing until their hair was plastered damp to their heads, while we watched.

We came home then, and dinner was ordinary. A roast and baked potatoes and asparagus. But the asparagus was fresh, and the Hollandaise lemony and not from a box, and everybody ate without a fuss, tired and ravenous and subdued from a day outside.

We stood outside in the twilight, before my dad headed back to Chicago, watching people bundle up the winter's fall of branches and leaves, listening to the clang of basketballs bounced by the teenagers across the street. We leaned back on our heels and strained to see, in the shadows, the places on the eaves that my father said needed painting. We said good-bye then, with hugs all around, and my father commented on the quality of the day.

"It was fine," he said. "It was beautiful."

It was an ordinary Sunday in the middle of the year and the

middle of my life, in the fullness of my father's, at the beginning of my children's.

It was an ordinary day, set apart by its quality of appreciation. It was experienced just as it happened, simply and fully, without strain or preoccupation or unmet agenda. It was one for the memory book that needs no pages, one to remember long after I forget the date.

The Christmas
Nobody Wanted

I can remember actually scolding my middle son when he was only about three years old for soiling his new white shirt just before we took our Christmas photos. Everything had to be perfect for our annual portrait of the four children—from the candy-cane-and-polar-bear wreath around the clock to the hat on the stone figure just inside the door. And in order to be perfect, everything had to be exactly the same as it had been the year before.

Tradition—it's something that you want your children to revere. When you carry on traditions, you try to keep things the same. But a few years ago, just as summer switched into high gear, something changed. My husband died.

Four months before, at forty-four, he'd been diagnosed with cancer. His illness was quick, but it was no more merciful than a brushfire. After he died, the months tumbled past as we sat palms upward, too numb to plan or to even recognize the shift of seasons. By the time Christmas rolled around, the five of us (myself, a daughter in college, a son in preschool, and two boys in the middle) knew one thing for sure: Nothing would ever be the same. Nothing I could do for the holidays could make them perfect again.

Still, there were holidays to make, a tree to cut, and the monumentally time-consuming Italian cookies to bake—a treat the children lusted for all year long. But I couldn't do all of that alone. So when my ten-year-old son, Bobby, suggested that we cut a new type of tree, the kind that sheds needles like a golden retriever sheds hair, I said, swallowing all my history,

"Fine." We hauled the tree home one bitterly cold day and set it up in the living-room window. It was about a foot too tall. (I'd never measured a tree without my husband before.) We got the shears and whacked some of it off.

"Perfect," said Bobby with a sidelong glance at me. "Do you think I sawed that tree down very well?"

"Very well," I told him. "Good as a grown-up."

When it was time to set up my heirloom-quality, hand-cast stone crèche, I stopped. For nearly twenty years, I had put it in the same place—centered on the mantel, surrounded by delicate star tinsel—then alternately admired and worried about it for a couple of weeks before taking it down. Throughout the past year, a soccer ball signed by my son Danny's seven-year-old teammates in honor of their late coach had occupied the sacred spot above the fireplace. Danny, who missed the coach (his late father) more than anyone else on the team, couldn't bear to move it. Instead, we put a string of lights around the soccer ball.

"Perfect," said Danny. And I agreed.

Long ago, I had explained to the children how, in France, families move the wise men closer to the manger each day throughout Advent, the four weeks leading up to Christmas, to symbolize their journey to the stable. We used to do the same thing with our little wooden children's crèche. But last year, I turned around one busy morning to find that my four-year-old had already set up the manger—his way. Along with Joseph, Mary, the Babe, and the wise men, the crèche featured Batman, Kermit, and a small green Apatosaurus. Fine by me. After all, wouldn't superheroes and giant beasts of the field have wanted to witness the holy sight, too?

My husband and I used to have a ritual brawl every year over the tree lights. He'd been of the "throw them up and see where they land" school; I wanted to twine each wire lovingly deep into a bough. The children were sidelined—not allowed to touch. Now everyone waded in to help. We all drooped and draped, more or less as high as we could reach. When we were done, all the white lights were on the top of the tree and all the red lights were on the bottom.

"Looks like a candy cane," I told my daughter the night she came home from college for winter break.

"Perfect," she said.

Well, it wasn't perfect. It wasn't the measured and stately and quite glorious holiday I took pride in stage-managing year after year. Those had been grand Christmases; this was a funky one. But the children had had a larger hand than ever before in creating it, a larger sense of owning it. Grief had made the choice for me, but I quickly saw the value of this Christmas. Every night before they went to bed, the younger kids would troop out to take another look at "their" lights— the fluorescent rainbow-colored electronic kind that buzz carols. I had to return one malfunctioning string four times. It never really worked, and even when it did, it sounded to me like the first eight bars of "Chewy, Chewy." To the boys it sounded like the music of angels. They liked it—that was what mattered.

This year, as we ready ourselves for another Christmas without the dad whose laugh alone could have halted border wars, we know that we still aren't fully healed, not fully grounded in new patterns.

But not every change has been for the worse. I wander through the mall, hearing voices raised in frustration. The paper store has already run out of the penguin print, someone moans. The candy canes for the intricate craft project are way too expensive, says another shopper. I remember that kind of detail and my concern for it. It showed caring, but in a way that hardly matters to me now.

I have come to believe that the Martha Stewart school of holiday observance—the effort to turn a celebration into a tableau into which people are fitted as neatly as hand-stenciled place mats—was wrong. And I was wrong, too.

I haven't given up on traditions; traditions are a thing we should respect. But they should be big frames in which ideas can be shifted and regrouped, not tight cross-stitched pictures. When children have a freer hand in shaping an event, they savor it more than they could ever savor joy presented to them on a platter.

And so I have resolved: As Batman on the roof of the manger is my witness, I will never again be the sole architect of a holiday. I haven't given up on doing things well, but I have given up trying to control the definition of what doing something well means. And I don't care any less than I used to. If anything, our revamped family holidays may teach my children the flexibility it really takes to care more. So they may grow up knowing what I needed to learn the hard way—that each holiday is precious simply for the privilege of having it, and thus perfect, in its own way.

Epilogue: The Prime of Miss Late Bloomer

YOU'RE, now, let's see ... how old?" the radio interviewer asked me, right there in front of God and thousands of listeners, opening a show that was supposed to be about books and authors, not about my odometer reading.

For a moment, a panic blip surfaced on my mind's screen.

"Lie," I thought. "Shave a couple of years. People do it all the time."

But I don't do it all the time, and I duly reported my forty-three years, and not just in the interest of truth. What I really hoped to send was the radio equivalent of a message in a bottle: I hoped that someone out there would raise her head and really listen. Maybe someone trying to ignore the roar of her seven-year-old's remote-control car while filling out a financial-aid application for college. Someone who's been told over and over that the expense of getting a degree wouldn't be worth the years she had left to use it. Maybe someone who finally realized she couldn't bear to see the sun come up through tears even one more time—that she was walking out, no matter what it would cost her. Or someone who thinks she's washed up, the edges of her star turning brittle on the beach, seeing love and success and joy no longer as horizon hopes but as keepsakes in a collection on a shelf. I figured that this someone might feel hopeful—hearing about my age, my widowhood, my five kids, and my not terribly prepossessing Midwestern way of life—that her own ambitions didn't have quite so many odds stacked against them as it may have seemed.

"So," the interviewer went on, "you're really too old for success to spoil your life, aren't you?"

Stinker, I thought.

But as I summoned up an answer, I realized that he was, perhaps for all the wrong reasons, absolutely right.

When the first novel I ever wrote became a surprise success last year, lots of people asked me something like, "Where have you been all your life?" It forced me to consider. Why had I waited so long? It wasn't simply lack of time or courage or desire, though certainly all those obstacles played their parts. If I were asked that question now, I'd have to say, feeling neither coy nor bitter, that I was getting ready. That I was never the fastest in the pack. That I wasn't the comet that took its arc up early and startled those around me. That asked, for a college yearbook story, what quality I valued most in people, I answered, "Endurance."

Was I actually glad, the radio guy wanted to know, that my time had arrived now, instead of fifteen years ago?

Glad? That isn't the way I'd put it. I'm not *glad* that success—and a whole banquet of other, unrelated and unexpected benefits—overtook me only in midlife.

Not glad, perhaps, but certainly content. And probably lucky. From my point of view, I'm lucky that my route to economic security—and other kinds of security—was a marathon instead of a sprint. Just as I'm lucky for the big cesarean scar on my stomach, a totem that signifies an event of more richness and complexity than I ever could have fully understood in my twenties.

Perhaps that wouldn't hold true for everyone. It does for me, however, because I'm a late bloomer.

My Aunt Patricia told me so when I was twelve, when I despaired of ever being anything but a mouthful of metal, renowned by boys only for her pathetic willingness to rewrite English assignments. I was told so in college, by a professor who said, when I dreamed of being a writer, "Right now, you're raw as wet paint. Talk to me in ten years. No, twelve." And so said the doctor, when I was thirty, and everyone on the block except for me was pushing a baby carriage.

In the fullness of time, my grandmother used to say; but even I never imagined time quite so full of opportunities for patience. I used to chafe with irritation and envy as others burst out of the gate into marriage, solid careers, and serious style. I considered myself the human version of my favorite shoes, a pair of plain brown clogs—useful, plain, a steady striver with no taps on my toes.

No wonder. I'd grown up in an era in which sooner was simply better. That may, indeed, feel the same in every era, but perhaps because Baby Boomers were the largest generation ever in American history, our youth was heralded as a force in part because of sheer numbers. The schism of generations over the drama of Vietnam fueled our collective sense of powerful possibility—all the more powerful if precocious. If long-haired young men and women in T-shirts, armed only with the righteous anger of their speech, could bring adults to their knees, what exactly was it that we were supposed to admit we were too young to know? I became a reporter while the concussive waves of the Watergate scandal still shook the land; hadn't it been young men who called their corrupt elders to account? The real go-getters moved on quickly, to exotic bureaus and complex assignments. What I was best at—small essays in my Sunday column—garnered much affection, but little acclaim.

It wasn't that I was ever rootless or unsuccessful. My husband and I survived our early lumps to work out a satisfying marriage; together, by birth and adoption, we had four children. As a newspaper columnist, speechwriter, and magazine journalist, I built a modest but thriving reputation, though I never gave it much credit. I thought of myself as a quick, careful hack, but a hack nonetheless. I should be careful to point out, though, that if this had turned out to be my life's peak, I wouldn't have been depressed. I was only sporadically blue and never ungrateful, even if I rarely operated on more than 40 percent of my available wattage. My physical self grew motherly, and then more motherly. My work life plateaued, as the things I did fell more and more into predictable slots.

And if my world had not imploded, I might be there still. After my husband's death from cancer not long after my fortieth birthday, I remember now wondering what I'd actually do with all the time I had to kill—the forty-odd years I might hope to live. Instead, it was because of what is ordinarily the most stifling and destructive emotion—fear—that my life took a radical course that proved something to me I once would have noticed only long enough to scorn, and it's this: It's acceptable, and perhaps even preferable, to hit your true life's stride right in the middle of it, or even afterward. A person can be happier, stronger, more successful, and more attractive in midlife than at any other time because, for some of us, the middle of life is when we actually have the makings for it.

Now, I know this sounds like a commercial for hair coloring. I was the first to sneer when gorgeous blondes who clearly owned home liposuction units said, "This is what forty looks like." When Shirley MacLaine gabbled on about the splendors of age and experience versus the anxieties of youth, all the while painted up as a parody of the apple-cheeked chorus girl she was in *Irma La Douce*, my flesh crawled. All that earnest nattering about the splendors of fulfillment in age just sounded like so much whistling in the dark. Why kid yourself? I was better off when gravity was my pal, and I could look like a million bucks on four hours' sleep. I was better off being remarkable in a professional setting simply by virtue of being the youngest one at the table.

And I believed that lie more firmly than my thighs would

ever be again, for a long while. I confused physical allure with other kinds of power and promise, until, in the fullness of time, I learned.

Perhaps it wasn't only me, and the (very) gradual burnishing of that raw-paint personality. In my midlife, the world seemed to have opened its arms more generously as well. The promise of a later harvest may have always been valid for some women, but those just ahead of me seemed to have redefined fortysomething before I got there. They called it differently from the way their parents did: as an age when someone could sanely contemplate a first marriage or a doctorate degree instead of plugging away a few years before retirement. I remembered the headlines twenty years ago when Judith Guest wrote her unsurpassed classic, *Ordinary People*. Everywhere, I read, she was acclaimed "a first-time novelist—and at forty!" I expected the same thing. I didn't get it. More was made of my determination than of my age, which, for me, was the best thing about the whole experience.

In fact, it had taken all my courage to even try to write the book, because I'd never felt such fears, fed by clear messages from those who loved my family most. Mature women with families to raise alone didn't take up novel writing. With my history and my slender means, running after rainbows was selfish, even callous. A mere handful of the many friends I can claim dared to advise me to take a dare. But they were the ones I listened to, also because of fear, fear of what that long leftover life would feel like if it revolved around nothing but sacrifice. It isn't always tragedy that jump-starts people. After a life of singular pain and great success in business, my friend Susie went back to school to get a degree to teach reading. She says she simply reached the point where she knew emotionally as well as intellectually that life was finite, and that all her someday cards needed either to be played out or put back in the deck.

For me, the time of most unexpected growth was after the book was published, and I had to decide how to conduct a new life that had tapped me on the shoulder after I thought the band had taken their instruments and left.

For the first time in my life, I had security, a sense of real ability, and more chances than I could have imagined. All good things, yes, but wouldn't the same roses have been as sweet with more bounce to enjoy them? I guess I don't think so, and that isn't simply a matter of someone who swears by Toyotas because she happens to drive one. What late bloomers get as compensation for their wait is savor—when life puts blossoms in our open hands, we know how to carry them without crushing them.

Some of the things we know just can't be known except by having more life on our bones.

One of those things is that we know what we want, which makes us more "foolproof" than our younger counterparts. If we're wise enough to trust the instincts we've developed, we—since we're often the parents, the lead teachers, or the senior staff members—have had long practice in analyzing data to reach decisions, in work and in ordinary life. We've seen opportunities come and seen them go, and observed that it's the road not taken that we regret the longest. Whether it's a business venture or a partnership, we're more equipped to see—and heed—the signs of disaster speeding toward us like headlights on a freight train. To knowing eyes, those warnings can't disguise themselves as harmless fireflies.

Moreover, we're better able to cope with success. Money may make the world go around, but it can rarely turn the head of a wise late bloomer; we've spent half a lifetime earning, spending, and learning to understand what money means—and what it doesn't. The road is littered with people who found success early, even prematurely, and foundered when they were seduced into thinking "price" was a measure of personal worth.

For a late bloomer, the big green reveals its true colors. It lets you go forward, and it tempers some basic worries, but we're not even tempted to waste it on the things we well realize it cannot buy. Those of us who have been in the marketplace longer don't really have to feel encroached upon by younger colleagues, not if we sharpen the focus of what we want from our lives. Older people simply know how to work better. We have greater experience and skills, more finesse and sophistication, and a sense of the culture of work, and this makes us more valuable—not to employers interested only in saving a buck by hiring less expensive cubs, but to those with taste. Such as maybe yourself.

I'm surrounded by friends who decided that turning forty meant permission to change their careers or become their own bosses. They've told me that they've grown more willing to take risks to achieve their dreams, because seeing life from the middle out reveals that it is both finite and ever-expanding.

It's astounding to see that, despite the cultural message we absorb all our lives—including that the key to maturity is settling for less—women still somehow remain more open to the future as they age than men do. We see all around us evidence that things, from climbing your first mountain to having your first child, are more possible, for a longer time, than previous generations ever realized. Loss may be even more profound for us now than it was when we were young, but those of us who hit our stride later in life rebound with more vigor from setbacks because we've ridden the waves before, and can remember times when we've had to simply ride them out without going under.

That's such an irreplaceable ability—resilience, the understanding that you can survive almost anything. I have heady days, and days when a good headache remedy is the best I can hope for. But it's with relish that I say that I've been around the block a time or two. I know life has topography, ups followed surely by downs. I once thought every setback was the knell of doom—that life without my wrecked car or my lost sweetheart, or even my best fingernail, wasn't worth the candle. But now my priorities are in better order. And as a result, there are few matters, material or personal, the loss of which would drive me to despair. One's in college and the other four are asleep upstairs.

Which doesn't mean I identify myself only as Mom, and have hung up my spurs as a woman. There was a time when a woman of my age might have been considered a dried flower on the vine of romance. But today I see all around me, in celebrity magazines and in my neighborhood, people falling in love well into their fifth decades and beyond, and not just cozy-companions-walking-in-the-park kind of love, either. And it's not only for unmarried moms such as I. People don't "retire" as early as they once did, and they're less likely to buy a van and drive to Sun City than to open their own coffeehouse. *The Bridges of Madison County* was pap on paper, but millions bought its message because that message was so robust. If you're single—or, as my aunt used to sweetly phrase it, "still single" only you can count yourself out. There are plenty of nights I go to sleep aching to put my head on the shoulder of a male taller than I who isn't also fourteen years old. But there is never a morning when I wake up prepared to compromise for companionship by risking deceit, abuse, or even boredom. I understand the uses of solitude and its limits, and what I'm willing to sacrifice for the blessing of companionship isn't what it used to be—which was everything. To be honest, men are not now lined up at my doors with bouquets. I interest fewer of them at my age, but those I interest are choice. All the bad kissers and belittlers are weeded out; they know they need not even apply. When I was younger, I thought a man in my life was the equivalent of oxygen. I still want a passion both sane and grand, but knowing that I can live without it may prove to be the best thing I ever learned about love.

Let's be honest. Short of sheep hormones and surgery, nothing is going to give me, a late bloomer, the flower freshness of Winona Ryder. But presence and style and confidence are powerfully sexy. And you aren't necessarily born with those things. In fact, getting to full bloom can be like getting to Carnegie Hall; it takes practice. Anjelica Huston is no baby, but she's a babe. She's her majesty, a grown woman. Because I don't have the metabolic grace of youth and the easy physical forgiveness of youth, I take great care to keep healthy from the bones out. As a result, I can outrun my kids. Do I cherish and revere the lines around my lips? No, I hate them. I know men notice them. Other women do, too. But at least I now realize, and I didn't when I was thirty, that I'm the one who notices them the most. Age is not just a matter of attitude; it's a plain fact. But only attitude—not skin cream—can really force back the presumption of age alone as a liability.

When I was in college, one of my favorite books was Muriel Spark's glowing, painful novel *The Prime of Miss Jean Brodie.* Stripped of her beauty and her romantic illusions, the aging teacher ruthlessly advances her own fantasies through her students. They do not understand her, she reminds them, for they are little girls, and she, Miss Brodie, is in her prime. It is not a sympathetic portrait, and for most of my life I considered its poignancy, if not its malice, the inevitable destiny for women of a certain age.

But now, I don't. For all the embarrassing things my generation has done in the name of sweet youth, Baby Boomers may at least have made the world safe for late bloomers. Having taken a tediously long time growing up, I see people around me similarly unwilling to set any speed records for growing old. Is this bad? It certainly makes for an energetic climate, and a challenge to our own children. My grandmother said it. Perhaps she could see that I was the kind of person who would only realize herself in the fullness of time. The point is, I don't think it was just a lucky accident that I waited until now to roll the dice, and had them come up lucky sevens. I think the exuberance of my second-act life is a trend, a fire sign for other Janie-come-latelies such as I—and there are plenty—as well as those poised to begin again. The lucky piece is that we're all set down in a time when there is suddenly room on the field of dreams not just for daffodils, which shoot up brave and bright through the earliest spring snow, but also for roses, which take their time, and last longer.